POLITICS
AND
MONEY

ALSO BY ELIZABETH DREW

Washington Journal: The Events of 1973–1974

American Journal: The Events of 1976

Senator

Portrait of an Election: The 1980 Presidential Campaign

POLITICS AND MONEY

THE NEW ROAD TO CORRUPTION

ELIZABETH DREW

MACMILLAN PUBLISHING COMPANY

New York

Macmillan Publishing Company
866 Third Avenue, New York, N.Y. 10022
Collier Macmillan Canada, Inc.

Most of the material in this book appeared originally in
The New Yorker, in slightly different form.

Library of Congress Cataloging in Publication Data

Drew, Elizabeth.
    Politics and money.

    1. Corruption (in politics)—United States.   2. Campaign
funds—United States—Corrupt practices.   3. Lobbying—
United States—Corrupt practices.   4. United States—Officials
and employees—Appointment, qualifications, tenure, etc.—
Corrupt practices.   5. Conflict of interests (Public office)—
United States.   6. United States. Congress—Ethics.   I. Title.
JK2249.D73   1983   320.973   83-7961

ISBN 0-02-533520-0

10   9   8   7   6   5   4   3   2   1

Printed in the United States of America

ACKNOWLEDGMENTS

The adventure of learning about the role of money in politics was the more rewarding for the help given me by a number of people. Some of them appear by name in this book; others, for obvious reasons, chose to remain anonymous. All of them taught me a lot, and did it with the mixture of insight, love of the lore, candid cynicism, patriotism, and humor that makes writing about politics such a fascinating pursuit. Some people cheerfully went to a great deal of trouble to help me; they know who they are, and that they have my gratitude.

I am also especially grateful to some people at *The New Yorker* who knocked themselves out to get the pieces from which this book originated into print on time: John Bennet, a gifted and enjoyable editor; Martin Baron; Nancy Franklin; and Ann Goldstein. And Kathy Glover, my assistant, was, as always, supportive and able. My husband, David Webster, can't type, but there is little else he didn't do to get me through this project.

—E. D.

AGAIN, FOR DAVID

INTRODUCTION

For some time, I had been interested in the role of money in the American political system. I had noticed, and heard politicians talk about, the pressures on them of raising money and the special access that large contributions procure. I had seen well-organized and well-armed interests—from various sectors of American life—win legislative victories and policy decisions at the expense of those less equipped to do battle. I understood that there would always be a competition among the interests within our country and that it would not always be a fair fight.

But in recent years, it became clear that the distortions of the system and the pressures on the politicians caused by money had grown to the point that they were making a qualitative change in the way the system worked. By the 1980s, the change was profound and disturbing. The most graphic and eloquent testimony to this effect came from the politicians themselves. And so, with the encouragement of William Shawn, the editor of *The New Yorker*, I set out to explore the ways that money is affecting our political system. What I found as I explored the subject was even more disturbing than what I had expected. This book is a fuller and updated account of what I wrote in *The New Yorker*.

While a good deal of attention has been paid to the growing costs of political campaigns, the real point is what the *raising* of the money to pay for those campaigns does to our politicians—and to our political system. It is driving the politicians into a new form of political corruption. It is making it very difficult for those who wish to avoid this corruption to do so. The pressures, real and imagined, on the politicians to raise large sums of money and to prevent large sums of money from being spent against them have become a full-time preoccupation on Capitol Hill, affecting the politicians' conduct of their job to a greater degree than ever. These pressures have provided new opportunities for the lawyers and lobbyists who try to shape national policies and have brought to their activities a new level of sophistication and a new energy. The pressures of money have made it more unlikely than ever that politicians will take difficult positions, exercise leadership. They have distorted the legislative product and the legislative process itself. The role of the legislator has changed. And the methods by which money is now organized and distributed have taken the country far from the way that our system of representative government is supposed to work.

I also found that there were great rivers of money that were essentially unaccounted for, and legally questionable, flowing into both our congressional and Presidential elections. Only a small group of political practitioners knew about them. Those rivers of money, plus other innovations, threaten to wreck the law providing public financing of Presidential campaigns, if they have not already done so. That law, which was intended to remove the influence of private money from Presidential politics, worked as it was supposed to in one election. Then a great deal of ingenuity went into finding ways around it.

There are things that can be done about all of this. The Presidential campaign law can be repaired. The influence of money on congressional behavior can be curbed. The American political system can be restored to the way it was supposed to work. At the end of this book, I offer some proposals to bring these things about; variations are of course possible. The point is not to try to establish a perfect system—even if we could define what that would be—but to bring us back closer to the fundamental principles of democracy. But before we can get there, we have to understand the nature of the problem.

ELIZABETH DREW
Washington, D.C.
March, 1983

POLITICS
AND
MONEY

The role that money is currently playing in American politics is different both in scope and in nature from anything that has gone before. The acquisition of campaign funds has become an obsession on the part of nearly every candidate for federal office. The obsession leads the candidates to solicit and accept money from those most able to provide it, and to adjust their behavior in office to the need for money—and the fear that a challenger might be able to obtain more. There are ostensible limits on how much can be contributed to candidates for the House and the Senate, but those limits are essentially meaningless. The law that established public financing of Presidential campaigns was intended to remove the role of private money from Presidential contests, but great rivers of private money, much of it untraceable, still flow into them. The only limits on how much money can be directed toward the election of a President are those on ingenuity.

The 1974 law setting limits on contributions to congressional and Presidential campaigns and establishing public financing for Presidential elections was finally enacted, after years of effort, amid the uproar over Watergate, when it was revealed that large, illegal corporate contributions had gone toward the election of Richard Nixon in 1972, that individuals had contributed enormous sums—the champion being W. Clement Stone, who contributed more than two million dollars—and that ambassadorships had been awarded to large contributors. But under the new laws there is nothing to prevent a W. Clement Stone from contributing a vast sum of money for the election of a Presidential candidate; he would simply have to go to more trouble to do so. A number of people did just that in the 1980 election. And ambassadorships and other high positions are still awarded to large contributors and fund raisers. The laws have given rise to "independent" committees working on a Presidential candidate's behalf which are independent in name only.

The political practitioners who have learned their way around both the Presidential and the congressional campaign-finance laws—and all the skilled ones have—view them with amusement. One Democratic practitioner says, "They are over-regulating the penguins on the tip of the iceberg." One Republican practitioner says the idea that there are any limits on the amounts of money that can flow into a Presidential campaign is "a myth." One oil lobbyist says that the idea that the law requiring the disclosure of funds contributed to congressional campaigns gives a real picture of the sources of the funds is "a joke." Senator Daniel Inouye, Democrat of Hawaii, says, "I think we're back about where we were before the laws were passed."

The result of all this is that the basis on which our system of representative government was supposed to work is slipping away, if it is not already gone. The role of the public representative has been changing dramatically in recent years. The processes by which Congress is supposed to function have been distorted, if not overwhelmed, by the role of money. The ability of even the best of the legislators to focus on broad questions, to act independently, or to lead has been seriously impaired. The race for money on Capitol Hill has turned into what one House member has described as "a fever" that has taken over the institution. The nature of the kind of person who might enter national politics is changing. Politicians who seek to enter, and do not have great wealth of their own to spend, are signed up on a systematic basis by interests that wish to enjoy influence over their official conduct. Many estimable people are concluding that they would prefer not to enter at all.

[2]

The Washington lobbyists and political consultants understand what is going on, and so do the politicians. "The key thing," says one lobbyist, "is what all this is doing to the way we govern ourselves. I think we're reaching the point where legislators make decisions only after thinking about what this means in terms of the money that will come to them or go to their opponents." A young lawyer-lobbyist says, "If you went into a typical senator's or congressman's office a few years ago, almost no one knew who the contributors were or who was coming to the fund-raisers. Now almost every staff member is involved: everybody is asked to give money, to get people to give money, to work on the fund-raising. The fact is that money is everything on the Hill these days. The change is overwhelming. When you talk to someone on Capitol Hill, inevitably the conversation turns to how much money the member has raised, where he's getting it, where he can get more." A Washington lawyer says, "Fund-raising has become a continuous activity."

Through the nineteen-fifties, everyone knew that sums of cash were in circulation, in exchange for legislation. The Bobby Baker scandal was just a symptom. The difference between then and now is one of approach and extent. Says a former Capitol Hill aide, "Now the politicians need more and more money; therefore, their threshold of principle is lower, and their willingness to compromise is greater. Everyone has learned that this is the way to do business." A number of members of Congress say they fear that some great scandal about money may be about to explode. In fact, that scandal may already be occurring. It takes the form not of one explosive event but of many often undramatic, everyday events. The search for one particular scandal misses the point. It is analogous to the search for the "smoking gun" during Watergate—the one clear example of criminality—in a landscape strewn with evidence of abuse of power.

The federal criminal statute makes it a crime to give or promise, or to ask for or receive, "anything of value" in exchange for any official act. The transactions between donors and politicians may stop short of such explicitness—though sometimes they do not—but the people involved in such transactions know the codes for getting around the letter, not to mention the spirit, of the law. Of course, not every contribution comes with a due bill, and not every politician is incapable of accepting a contribution and exercising independent judgment. And many contributions are made because the contributor already agrees with the candidate's point of view. But the pressures to gather large amounts of money are so great that the legislative process is inherently distorted, even corrupted, by the phenomenon. The effect of money on the legislative process takes several forms, some of them seemingly, but not actually, contradictory, and many, if not most, of them hidden from view. Because of the need for money or the fear of a well-financed opponent, a member of Congress might vote a certain way on a piece of legislation, or might try to avoid a vote on the matter, or might even forestall congressional consideration of it altogether. The effect might be in some action in a subcommittee, or some message to a colleague, that does not come to light. Legislation that in the earlier years might not have ever been seriously considered but has the backing of a particularly well-financed interest group can go whizzing through Congress. Other legislation, often involving important issues, can be so caught in the tangle of competing interests that Congress is paralyzed.

Until the problem of money is dealt with, it is unrealistic to expect the political process to improve in any other respect. It is not relevant whether every candidate who spends more than his opponent wins—though in races that are otherwise close, this tends to be the case. What matters is what the chasing of money does to the candidates, and to the victors' subsequent behavior. The candidates' desperation for money and the interests' desire to affect public policy provide a mutual opportunity. The issue is not how much is spent on elections but the way the money is obtained. The argument made by some that the amount spent on campaigns is not particularly bothersome, because it comes to less than is spent on, say, advertising cola, or purchasing hair-care products, misses the point stunningly. The point is what *raising* money, not simply spending it, does to the political process. It is not just that the legislative product is bent or stymied. It is not just that well-armed interests have a head start over the rest of the citizenry—or that often it is not even a contest. It is not just that citizens without organized economic power pay the bill for the successes of those with organized economic power. It is not even relevant which interests happen to be winning. What is relevant is what the whole thing is doing to the democratic process. What is at stake is the idea of representative government, the soul of this country.

2

There have always been "interests" in this country which have sought to influence public policy, and there always will be, and always should be. Legislators have to look after the various interests of the area they represent and work out the political equation among their constituencies. In *The Federalist Papers*, Madison wrote of the natural inclination of man to form factions, and said that the consequent "instability, injustice, and confusion introduced into the public councils have, in truth, been the mortal diseases under which popular governments have everywhere perished." Since to remove the causes of "the mischiefs of faction" would be to destroy liberty, Madison wrote, the alternative was to control their effects. He offered the hope that in the republican form of government which was being established, the number of conflicting factions would make it difficult for any particular one to dominate, or for those with a "common motive" to "discover their own strength and to act in unison with each other." But, realistic as Madison was, he could only extrapolate from the society he saw and, happily for him, could not anticipate the sophisticated organizing of almost every conceivable interest, the skills that factions would develop in promoting such interests, and the systematized raising and contributing of large sums of money in order to influence public policy.

In earlier periods of our history, some nationally based interests—steel, the railroads—assumed that it was only prudent business practice to own legislators and to influence the election of Presidents. Some of the more energetic fund raisers were awarded Cabinet positions and ambassadorships—a tradition that has not exactly died. The scandals over the power of the trusts, and over the manipulations of Mark Hanna, the Ohio mining magnate who was responsible for the nomination of William McKinley in 1896 and, for a time, literally for the fortune of the Republican Party, were factors leading to the reform movement of the early twentieth century. Hanna, a pioneer in the field, raised millions for the Republican Party by systematically assessing banks and corporations. Robert La Follette's reform movement grew out of these scandals, and it was in reaction to them that President Theodore Roosevelt made some farseeing proposals. In a message to Congress in 1905, Roosevelt proposed that all corporate contributions to politics be banned. In 1907, he went further, and proposed the public financing of campaigns, saying, "The need for collecting large campaign funds would vanish if Congress provided an appropriation for the proper and legitimate expenses of each of the great national parties. Then the stipulation should be made that no party receiving campaign funds from the Treasury should accept more than a fixed amount from any individual subscriber or donor; and the necessary publicity for receipts and expenditures could without difficulty be provided." In 1907, Congress passed the Tillman Act, which prohibited corporations and banks from making contributions to campaigns for federal office, and over the next few years Congress passed some fairly toothless legislation requiring the filing of reports of certain campaign contributions. Then, in 1921, came the Teapot Dome scandal, leading to the Federal Corrupt Practices Act of 1925, which continued the existing prohibitions on contributions by corporations and banks, and required the reporting of campaign receipts and expenditures, but the law was infinitely evadable and was never really enforced.

By 1970, there was such consternation over the rising costs of campaigns—political advertising on television had now become commonplace—that Congress passed a bill to limit the amount that could be spent for television and radio advertising, but Richard Nixon vetoed the measure, siding with broadcasters, who argued that it discriminated against them. The following year, Congress came close to completing action on a more comprehensive bill, which required, among other things, that all federal candidates disclose the sources of their campaign funds, but its final enactment was delayed until 1972, so that members of Congress and Presidential candidates could raise more money before the new disclosure requirements went into effect. The 1971 law dealt with what were seen as major problems at that time by limiting the amount that candidates (and their families) could spend on their own campaigns—there had been a couple of notable spenders in 1970—and limiting the amount that candidates could spend on political advertising. It also came at the question of costs from another direction, by requiring that television and radio stations charge their lowest rates for political advertising in the periods immediately preceding primaries and general elections. Common Cause, the citizens' lobby, which had been founded in 1970 and had made campaign financing one of its major issues, tried to get Congress to enact a limit on contributions, but the idea met with little interest.

At the same time, organized labor took the first of a series of steps to secure its own role in the political process—steps that led ultimately to the universe of political-action committees, or PACS. In 1972, labor leaders asked Congress to simply codify what was then understood to be existing law. Labor unions and corporations had been specifically barred from making direct contributions to political campaigns, but the law had been interpreted to mean that labor could use dues and corporations could use treasury funds to administer political committees that would raise voluntary contributions from their members or employees for the election of candidates for public office. In the nineteen-forties, labor had begun to establish political-action committees, to try to offset unlimited contributions by wealthy individuals. A few trade and professional associations had also established political-action funds—the American Medical Association, the dairy cooperatives, and something called the Business-Industry Political Action Committee, or BIPAC, which was founded in 1963. (BIPAC was begun by the National Association of Manufacturers in response to the A.F.L.-C.I.O.'s Committee on Political Education, or COPE.) And a very few corporate political-action committees had been set up. But labor was concerned that its right to establish political-action committees would be challenged by the Nixon Administration's Justice Department, so it backed an amendment to the 1971 bill which stated that the prohibition of direct contributions of treasury money by unions and corporations did not prevent them from establishing PACS using voluntary contributions. The amendment also said that union dues and corporate-treasury money could be used for "nonpartisan" get-out-the-vote drives and for communicating with members and stockholders about politics. Labor failed to consider that business had the resources to overtake it.

Not long afterward, in the course of the Watergate disclosures, it became clear that many corporations hadn't needed to establish political-action committees because they were maintaining secret funds for the financing of federal campaigns. The public was scandalized by such revelations as that Nixon's campaign committee, the Committee for the Re-Election of the President, had raised almost seventeen million dollars from only a hundred and twenty-four contributors, who gave more than fifty thousand dollars each, and that over $1.7 million had been received from people who were given ambassadorships.

And so in 1973 Congress went at the subject of campaign financing again, and in 1974 it passed the comprehensive law providing for the public financing of Presidential campaigns (the Senate had also approved public financing of congressional campaigns, but this was blocked in the House); placing limits on contributions by individuals and committees for all campaigns for federal office; limiting overall expenditures by congressional as well as Presidential campaigns (this replaced the 1971 ceiling on political advertising); and prohibiting expenditures by individuals and groups outside campaigns—independent expenditures. Cash contributions of over a hundred dollars were prohibited—an important restriction. A Federal Election Commission was established to enforce the federal election laws. The 1974 limits on independent expenditures, the overall spending limits on congressional campaigns, and the 1971 limit on spending by individual candidates using their own funds were later struck down by the Supreme Court (*Buckley v. Valeo*); in essence, the Court equated freedom of speech with the spending of money.

Two widely held misconceptions about what happened in 1974 are that the provision in the law which gave political-action committees their great sendoff was backed only by labor, and that its consequences were unforeseen. The provision was in fact a joint effort by labor and business. (The U.S. Chamber of Commerce and BIPAC, among others, were involved.) It stemmed from a suit brought by Common Cause in 1972 against the T.R.W. corporation, which had established a political-action committee. The suit was brought under a section of the Corrupt Practices Act which prohibited government contractors from making direct or indirect campaign contributions. T.R.W. dissolved the fund, and the suit was dropped. But labor, which had contracts with the government to train workers, became alarmed, and, joined by business, nearly succeeded in 1972 in rewriting that section of the law to allow government contractors to have PACs. In 1974, they succeeded.

Fred Wertheimer, the president of Common Cause, says, "The PAC provision was part of a much larger fight, but we as well as labor and business were paying attention to it. We could see that we were establishing a dual system, with public financing of Presidential campaigns and private financing of congressional campaigns. We knew where we were headed."

On December 31, 1974, there were approximately six hundred political-action committees. By November, 1982, there were about thirty-four hundred—an increase of almost five hundred percent. Between 1980 and 1982 alone, there was an increase of twenty-five percent. In 1976, political-action committees spent about twenty-three million dollars on congressional races. In 1982, they contributed about eighty million dollars—an increase of forty-five percent over two years earlier, and a total increase of two hundred and forty-eight percent in six years. And in each succeeding election, PACS have contributed a higher percentage of the winners' funds. In 1982, the average House winner received over a third of his money from PACS; more than one hundred members received over half of their funds from PACS. In 1974, there were eighty-nine corporate PACS; by 1982 there were fourteen hundred and ninety-seven, while labor had three hundred and fifty. Trade associations, such as the A.M.A. and the National Association of Realtors, had six hundred and and thirteen political-action committees. The rest were PACS maintained by "independent" groups, by cooperatives, and by single-interest ideological groups.

There were attempts—in 1976, 1977, and 1978—to legislate public financing of congressional campaigns; some came close in one chamber or the other, but all of them ultimately failed. In 1979, the House of Representatives passed legislation to limit to seventy thousand dollars the overall amount that a House candidate could accept from PACS. The legislation was not brought to the floor in the Senate, because Republican leaders threatened to conduct a filibuster against it.

One person who saw the possibilities of the 1974 law was Guy Vander Jagt, who in 1975 became the chairman of the National Republican Congressional Committee—the campaign committee for electing Republicans to the House. Vander Jagt, a representative from Michigan, says, "In 1975, I spent most of the year trying to get businesses and industries to establish PACS. I worked with the Chamber of Commerce and with the National Association of Manufacturers, and I travelled the country giving my Paul Revere speech: 'Wake up, America, wake up. There's a war going on—a war that will determine the economic future of this country, and you aren't involved.' " His cry of alarm was clearly heeded.

3

The general impression is that individuals may contribute only a thousand dollars, and political-action committees five thousand dollars, to a candidate for each office. In fact, the actual limits are quite a bit higher. The law allows individuals to contribute a thousand dollars to a given congressional candidate in a primary, in a runoff, and in a general election—a total of three thousand dollars. If a state party holds a convention as well as a primary and a runoff, a person can give four thousand dollars. Moreover, the Federal Election Commission has ruled that merely getting on the ballot for the general election can count as having a primary, and so any candidate can receive at least two thousand dollars from an individual. The law also allows an individual to give five thousand dollars to a political-action committee each year and twenty thousand dollars to a political party each year, and allows an individual's spouse and children to give the same amounts. While the law sets a limit of twenty-five thousand dollars on total individual contributions to all federal candidates during each two-year election cycle, the careful planner can manage to give fifty thousand dollars to candidates and committees per two-year cycle. (He does this by giving twenty-five thousand to parties and committees in the first year, and twenty-five thousand to candidates in the second.) He can give both to a candidate and to a PAC that he knows will contribute to that candidate.

There are two kinds of political-action committees: those established by corporations, trade associations, and labor unions;

and those established independently, usually with an ideological bent. The rules for establishing and running PACs are set forth in the law and in rulings by the Federal Election Commission. All that is legally required to create a PAC is a filing with the F.E.C. of a statement containing certain information. Contributions to, and by, PACs must also be reported to the F.E.C. Corporations and unions may pay the full cost of maintaining PACs and soliciting funds for them, and may take the money to do this from corporate or union treasury funds (money that cannot legally be spent in federal campaigns). Corporations may solicit contributions to their PACs from their executive and administrative personnel and from stockholders—and their families. Labor unions may solicit from members and their families. There are regulations designed to protect employees and union members from pressures to contribute, but the pressures, subtle and otherwise, exist. A separate set of regulations governs solicitations by trade associations. To qualify as a "multi-candidate committee," and thus be permitted to make contributions of five thousand dollars per candidate per election, a PAC must have been registered with the F.E.C. for at least six months, must have received contributions from at least fifty individuals, and must have made contributions to at least five federal candidates. (If a PAC has not qualified as a multi-candidate committee, it may contribute only one thousand dollars per candidate per election.)

The law allows a political-action committee to contribute five thousand dollars to a candidate for each primary, runoff, and general election, so each candidate can receive at least ten thousand dollars from a PAC. Moreover, many of the political-action committees work together, guiding and coordinating their contributions, and their combined effect on a campaign can be even more substantial. (A few PACs engage in what is called "bundling"—collecting checks made out to specific candidates from individuals—and thus they can in effect get around the five-thousand-dollar limit. This practice is under legal challenge.) PACs can contribute amounts up to five thousand dollars to an unlimited number of other PACs. If an individual or a PAC did not bet on the person who happened to win the primary or the general election, he or it has an opportunity to compensate later for this lack of foresight. One hears a lot about campaign debts, but it turns out that they are not unintentional. Robert Keefe, a man with considerable experience as a Democratic Party official and consultant, says, "A smart politician will always have a bookkeeping debt from his primary, so that he can be sure that people who want to give him more money will have an opportunity. The same thing is true for the final election. You have to be very creative in your bookkeeping. Besides, you can spend for things in your primary that will help you in your final. Then, if you're a contributor and you gave to the wrong guy, you have an opportunity to become retroactively smart."

An industry can provide money both through PACs and through individual contributions, so tracing the PAC contributions provides only part of the picture of the money that flows to politicians. For example, an oil lobbyist told me he estimated that only about a third of the independent-oil industry's contributions are made through PACs. This is the lobbyist who calls the Federal Election Commission listings "a joke." There is no way to determine from the F.E.C. reports the business interests of all those who are listed as individual contributors. The listings say things like, "Joe Smith, businessman, Tulsa," or "Steve O'Brien, self-employed, Washington, D.C." (The term "self-employed" often indicates a lawyer—especially in Washington, D.C.) An individual may well contribute both through a PAC and on his own. And some politicians who make a big point of their refusal to accept money from PACs have no compunctions about accepting it from individuals who contribute to PACs. One House member said, "We all try to raise money from people who also give to PACs."

There are still other, and even less well-known, routes for directing money into campaigns. There is what those versed in ways of collecting and directing campaign funds call "soft money," one of the least noticed and understood conduits for campaign funds. "Hard money" is money that the parties and candidates raise in individual contributions or from political-action committees. But the parties have found a way to arrange for money that cannot be directly contributed to federal elections—union dues, corporate-treasury funds, or individuals' contributions beyond the legal limits—to be used for certain of their activities. (The money can come right out of a corporation's treasury, thus enabling a businessman to contribute his stockholders' money instead of his own.) Its origin was in a 1979 change in the law which allowed the state parties to raise funds for certain minor election activities (the purchase of pins, bumper stickers, and so on) and, more important, for get-out-the-vote drives for Presidential campaigns. These were given the high-minded term "party-building activities."

The theory was that the state parties should be able to participate in the publicly financed Presidential campaign. In many states, including some of the most populous ones, the laws allow union and corporate-treasury money, plus unlimited individual expenditures, to be used for political activities. But in 1980 the national parties assumed the role of raising and distributing such funds—which was not the intent of the law—and have significantly expanded their use. Through an imaginative, and questionable, interpretation of the law, both parties now use soft money for congressional as well as Presidential campaigns. They use it as much as they can—and as much as they think they can get away with—for television advertising and for get-out-the-vote drives. Their rationale is that they are using soft money for non-federal elections—for governorships, state legislatures, and so on. (The only federal election mentioned in the 1979 change in the law was the one for President.) But, obviously, efforts to motivate people to vote for the party ticket at the state level are likely to benefit the candidates for federal office as well. So the distinction is a false one, and the lengths to which the parties go to make distinctions between their soft-money and hard-money expenditures are fairly ludicrous.

In 1982, both parties used soft-money contributions from corporations, unions, and individuals for campaigns in various states. The only limits on how much soft money can go into a state are those imposed by the states themselves, and they are varied, and in some cases nonexistent. In addition, none of this money has to be reported at the federal level. The Republicans, inevitably, raise most of their soft money from corporations, and the Democrats, inevitably (but not solely), from labor. Some of the Democrats' soft money, like some of the Republicans', comes from wealthy contributors who agree to give the parties more than they are allowed to under the federal limits. One Democratic official says, "We have to constantly remind people that they aren't bound by the federal election law." A Democratic activist in Washington said to me, "I could write a check tomorrow for the Party for one million dollars and put it all in soft money." Similarly, Richard Bond, the deputy chairman of the Republican National Committee, said, "If Mobil Oil wanted to give you twenty million bucks, I think they could give you twenty million bucks, and you don't have to show it." He added, "I'm not aware of any such sugar daddy."

Both parties use the money to help pay for ads that are run in states where soft money is legal. In some cases, the Democratic and Republican National Committees establish state accounts for the purpose of funnelling in soft money. The whole exercise keeps the committees' lawyers busy. Bond says, "When we have a state we want to give soft money in, we'll run it down to our lawyer and ask how we put it in." Some lawyers familiar with the election laws question the legality of both parties' using soft money in such ways; they think that to collect and spend on a national basis money that can legally be used only at the state level is out-of-bounds. Says a former F.E.C. official, "It would be one thing if the money were raised in Illinois and spent in Illinois. But for it to be raised in Washington and spent in Illinois is legally questionable." The Democratic activist, a lawyer, said that despite all the rationalizations the effect of the expenditures is to help national candidates. Therefore, he said, both parties' use of soft money is "illegal as hell." The 1982 elections were the first congressional elections in which the national committees got into the soft-money business in any substantial way. But unless the rules are changed this questionable use of unreportable money is, like other innovative uses of money in politics, likely to expand.

In 1982, the Republicans used soft money to pay for some ads urging people to vote Republican. One ad that was paid for with soft money in, for example, California said that times are tough, but Reagan has cut inflation, so give the guy a chance. This ad, it was explained, was not on behalf of any candidate for federal office. In California, the national Party could not use soft money to advocate the election of Pete Wilson for senator, but it could do so for the election of George Deukmejian for governor. But, obviously, if the ad helped Deukmejian, it helped Wilson. The tortuous reasoning that went into some of the Democratic Party's decisions on how to use soft money shows how ridiculous the distinctions are. The Democrats ran ads on "trickle down" economics which were paid for with hard money because, their lawyers ruled, that was a federal issue. But their ad showing an elephant named Dixie smashing up a china shop was paid for with both hard (twenty-five percent) and soft (seventy-five percent) money, according to the issue printed on the plate she smashed ("Social Security," "State and Local Taxes," "Jobs"). The reasoning was that the ad's tag line—"The Republicans have made a mess of things. Now they want to throw their weight around our state"—justified paying for it with soft money, except in the case of the plate marked "Social Security," which was a purely federal issue. An ad on unemployment was paid for with soft money on the ground that if a person was unemployed, he would go to the state unemployment office.

The Democrats used soft money to pay for spots in several states that had gubernatorial races—and also Senate and House races—they wanted to help. For example, they used soft money to buy a spot in Illinois, ostensibly to help Adlai Stevenson III in his race for the governorship, but the spot was run in Peoria, where the Democrats were in fact hoping to defeat Robert

Michel, the House Minority Leader. (Another gambit both parties resort to is using soft money to buy media time in areas whose media markets reach into states that don't allow soft money.) Republicans, especially in the closing days of the campaign, sent large amounts of soft money—through their own contributors and through allied groups—into California, where the defeat of Jerry Brown, the Democratic candidate for the Senate, meant a great deal to the Reagan White House. (Brown lost.) They sent soft money into other close races at the end as well. The Democrats, harder pressed than the Republicans for funds of any sort, admitted to raising and spending about three to four million dollars in soft money in 1982, but they were heavily outspent in hard money. For the well-off Republican Party, soft money is a way of getting around the limits on what it can do for its candidates directly; for the Democrats, for whom meeting the limits is a distant dream, it is a way of raising money.

Under the law, the national parties may make large direct contributions to their candidates for the House and Senate. A provision allowing national or state parties to spend certain amounts per voter was put in the 1974 law in order to allow the parties to spend above the limits that the law set for candidates for all federal offices. When the Supreme Court, in the Buckley case, struck down the limits for all but the Presidential campaign, this provision was left in the law. In 1975, the Republicans got a ruling from the F.E.C. that permitted them to combine federal and state expenditures—thus allowing them to pour enormous amounts of money into certain states under these "coordinated expenditures." About fifty thousand dollars could be put into each House race. By 1980, they had built this into a major activity. The Republicans, being far better at raising money, were able in both 1980 and 1982 to put large amounts into the states—while the Democrats did not come close. In 1980, the Republicans were poised with so much money that, for example, in New York, right after the September primary they were able to commit over seven hundred thousand dollars to Alfonse D'Amato, their senatorial candidate, while the Democrats spent twenty-five thousand for his opponent, Elizabeth Holtzman, who was still paying off her primary debt. D'Amato won. In all, in 1980 the Democrats helped their Senate candidates directly with a total of five hundred and ninety thousand dollars; the Republicans shelled out to their Senate candidates a little over five million dollars. In 1982, the Democratic Senatorial Campaign Committee contributed $2.3 million to its candidates, and its Republican counterpart contributed $9.2 million. And in 1980 the Republican National Committee was wealthy enough to run a year-long national "generic" advertising campaign, stressing that it was "time for a change"—a campaign that helped make all Democratic incumbents vulnerable. In 1982, it began running its generic ads in May. The Democratic National Committee didn't run national ads in either year.

4

The amount of money that is now available for political campaigns has had a profound effect on the legislators, and the effect became particularly striking in the Ninety-seventh Congress, which met in 1981–82. The use of political-action-committee money and party money in the 1980 election raised to a new level the "fear factor" governing congressional behavior. Traditionally, PACs had played it safe, and had given the great proportion of their money to incumbents, whether the incumbents were in any electoral danger or not—especially if they were not. And since Democrats were in the majority in Congress, a substantial amount of PAC money went to Democrats. But in 1980 a combination of persuasion by Republican Party leaders and seizing of opportunity by the managers of PACs led to an unprecedented amount of PAC money going to candidates who were challenging incumbents. The exercise was successful on two levels: it helped defeat some incumbents, and it scared the daylights out of incumbents who survived. What the survivors saw was that business PACs, whose numbers were growing, were more willing to back a challenger, particularly in a close race. Now it was a question not just of how much money one could raise but of how much money might go to one's opponent.

William Brock, the Republican National Committee chairman from 1977 until 1981, said to me in the fall of 1982, "The PACs are supporting challengers more. We really worked on that in 1980. We said, 'The business of business is to take risks.' We managed to get PACs to give a third of their money to challengers." In 1980, most of the incumbent Democratic senators were able to raise more money overall for their campaigns, but the Republicans were able to narrow the gap, as a result of the combination of PAC money, substantial spending on the candidates' behalf by the Republican Party, and spending against the Democrats by independent committees. The champion PAC-money raiser in 1980 was Charles Grassley, Republican of Iowa, who raised more than seven hundred thousand dollars from PACs in his successful effort to defeat the incumbent senator, John Culver. And three other successful Republican Senate challengers ranked after Grassley as PAC-money raisers. A great deal of Grassley's money came from oil interests and chemical interests, after Culver had guided through Congress a bill requiring these companies to contribute to a "superfund" to clean up toxic-waste sites. Grassley's political-action-committee director was quoted in the New York Times in 1980 as saying, "In the early morning, we start calling the East Coast PACs, and we work across the country with the sun." In 1982, a higher proportion of the PAC money went to incumbents than it had in 1980. The champion PAC-money raiser in 1982 was Pete Wilson, Republican of California, who defeated Governor Jerry Brown in a race for the Senate. Wilson became the first candidate to raise a million dollars from PACs.

Moreover, much of the 1980 money came in at the last minute, taking the incumbents by surprise. Leon Panetta, a Democratic representative from California, says, "In the past, Democrats tried to stress individual contributions by citizens in the area, and labor was good for some money. But labor couldn't expand its ability to raise money, while business was mushrooming. In the 1980 election, we could see that a Republican challenger had the ability to get two or three hundred thousand dollars in the last weeks of the campaign and knock off the incumbent. There were a lot of examples of that, and it scared the Democrats to hell." David Obey, a Democratic representative from Wisconsin, talking of the last-minute money phenomenon, says, "If members know that that can happen to them, it means they will be looking over their shoulder every damn vote. It forces them to raise war chests that can be sitting there for the last-minute onslaught. If you're on a committee with jurisdiction over big interests, you can be sure of raising a lot of money. If you're not—if you're just dealing with problems—you don't have that assurance, and you may be defined as a seat the other party can pick up, and *boom!* It just forces people to spend an incredible amount of time on fund-raising." All this had its effect on the Congress that convened in January, 1981. Says Panetta, "It's one of these things that always float beneath the surface. Sometimes you think a vote will go a certain way and it goes another, and you can't figure it out for a moment. Then you learn that it was money." Both Obey and Panetta said before the 1982 elections that they suspected that movements of large amounts of money into Republican campaigns were being coordinated somewhere in Washington. They were correct.

5

Once a week beginning in January, 1982, a group that called itself "the assets-and-priorities group" met at the White House to decide which would be the targeted races in November, and to allocate to those races whatever assets the White House could call upon. Those assets were, of course, considerable. Lee Atwater, the deputy assistant to the President for political affairs, talked to me on a September afternoon in 1982 about the unprecedented White House coordination of political money. Atwater was thirty-one at the time, and an enthusiastic former academic from South Carolina who had worked in the 1980 Reagan Presidential campaign. Atwater, sitting in a well-furnished office in the Executive Office Building, told me that the White House had never before been used properly as the "central coordinating unit" in off-year elections.

Those who attended the meetings of the assets-and-priorities group included Atwater; the staff directors of the Republican House and Senate campaign committees; Edward Rollins, the White House Political Director; and Rich Bond, of the Republican National Committee. A few others floated in and out. The targeted races were constantly scrutinized for how the Republican candidates were doing and what might be helpful. (Races were moved off or onto the list; at one point or another, some sixty-five races were targeted.) "There's never been a political shop here before that did nothing but this," Atwater said. (The Reagan White House claims to be the first one to have a full-time, officially designated political director.) "This is what we've done for two years." Among the assets the group could offer, of course, were visits by Cabinet members and other luminaries. The Secretary of the Treasury was quite valuable: "Don Regan coming into a district is worth thirty, thirty-five thousand dollars in money-raising," Atwater said. He put the value of a visit by Vice-President Bush at between thirty-five and a hundred thousand dollars. The Reagan White House, for all its disdain for federal handouts, was no more reluctant than its predecessors to deliver federal favors to key electoral areas. But this sort of thing is traditional and routine. Among the innovations by the Reagan White House was an eighteen-second television shot of each of the Republican candidates for the House, the Senate, and governor talking to President Reagan, to be used in a thirty-second spot. "It looks like the guy lives here," Atwater said.

The most important innovation, however, was the Reagan White House use of political-action committees. Atwater said, "The big story of the campaign is that this is the first time the White House has really been involved with the political-action committees since their birth. Carter didn't really do anything with them. We have a full-time PAC operation at the Republican National Committee, under Rick Shelby. A lot of PAC money will be dumped in the targeted races toward the end—between seventy-five and two hundred and fifty thousand dollars. You add that to the nearly fifty thousand dollars the Republican National Committee and the congressional committee combined can give to a House candidate, plus the thirty thousand dollars that can be raised by a Cabinet officer's visit, and you get a total of three hundred and thirty thousand dollars. This is money outside the district that we're making sure they get. We're making sure that everyone gets from a hundred and fifty to four hundred grand extra, and that's a big wallop out there in a congressional district. Much of the PAC money will have already gone in, but there will be an extra spring there at the end."

I asked Atwater how the coordination of the PAC contributions worked.

He replied, "The congressional campaign committee and the Republican National Committee are having meetings with every PAC in town and saying, 'Here's the targeted list sanctioned by the R.N.C., the congressional committee, and the White House.' " The Republican congressional and senatorial campaign committees also held briefings for PACs in several cities outside Washington.

I asked Atwater what he thought the impact of all the money the Republicans could put into an election would be.

He replied, "I've got to think that the money and all the other resources combined will be worth about two percentage points for about thirty candidates. I think the story of this off-year election is that we've marshalled our resources and bought one or two Senate seats and fifteen to twenty House seats, and that's really good."

As things turned out, the Republicans lost twenty-six House seats. Republican Party officials themselves said that if it hadn't been for the money the losses would have been greater. The two parties broke even in the Senate, but a switch of about seventy thousand votes in five states would have given those seats to the Democrats. In all of these states but one (Nevada, where a Democratic incumbent senator lost), the winner outspent the loser. In fact, the winners outspent the losers in twenty-seven of the thirty-three Senate races. In five of the six races where the margin of victory was four percent or less, the winners spent twice as much as the losers.

During the last two weeks of the campaign, the Republican committees were able to put, and steer, large amounts of money into close races. Nancy Sinnott, the executive director of the National Republican Congressional Committee, told me after the election that all the Republican committees combined were able to spend approximately fifty million dollars in the final weeks. She said that toward the end her committee was able to go into a congressional district quickly with a new television ad, or could buy more television time. "We may have stemmed the tide through that," she said. The National Republican Senatorial Committee was well-financed enough to invest in "tracking" polls, which kept tabs on close races on a daily basis. The information thus obtained, plus the money Republicans were able to spend following up with television ads and mail appeals, was credited with saving some Republican incumbents. And the soft money went in, and the PAC money went in. In October of 1982, when White House aides began to prepare the public for a loss of some thirty Republican House seats, the Republican National Committee was saying that the loss would be only about twelve; the committee was deliberately trying to keep the PACS enthusiastic about supporting its candidates. At the end, the Republicans' effort was no longer directed at upsetting Democrats but at trying to protect incumbents—what one Republican official called an "enclave strategy."

The two parties headed into the election with a substantial imbalance in the treasuries of their national, Senate, and House committees. As of the reports filed June 30th, the last date of such committee filings before the election, the Democratic Party committees together had raised twenty-four million dollars, and the Republicans had raised a hundred and sixty-one million. The final figures for the year showed that the Democratic Party committees had spent twenty-seven and a half million dollars, and the Republicans had spent one hundred eighty-six and a half million. The National Republican Congressional Committee was so well-to-do that it had direct computer links with forty campaigns. Moreover, the Republican committees were in a position to provide, through their combined resources, the maximum amount allowed by law in direct contributions to each of the candidates the Party considered a priority. The Republicans were thus able to tempt people to run. Moreover (and to the relief of the Party leaders), most of the candidates had been recruited in 1981, before the Reagan record threatened to be a liability. "We locked them in with our resources," Bond told me. In addition to money, the Party could provide training, press assistance, and so on.

The Republican Party's wealth stems in part from the large

resources of its historic business constituency and in part from the direct-mail fund-raising it began in 1965, starting with the ideological conservatives who constituted Barry Goldwater's following. The Republicans like to talk about the high percentage of their funds that come from the "small contributors" through direct mail, and know that it is good politics to portray themselves as the party of "small donors." The Democrats, on the other hand, have tried direct mail only fitfully, and have in fact relied on labor and a few wealthy businessmen. The Democrats didn't have the discipline to reinvest the proceeds sufficiently to build a strong direct-mail operation. Starting in 1981, they tried again, but the process takes years.

When Atwater was explaining to me how the PAC contributions are coordinated, he said, "Rick Shelby, over at the R.N.C., is the guy who actually does all that. The reality is that everyone knows that Shelby and I have worked together for years. People know that Shelby is not over there pulling races out of thin air." Shelby worked with some two hundred and twenty-five PACs, guiding their investments. Atwater further explained that Shelby was also working with a group headed by two influential Republicans—William Timmons, a major Republican Washington lobbyist, and Clark MacGregor, a former chairman of the Committee for the Re-Election of the President. Timmons worked in the White House under Nixon and Ford as the assistant to the President for legislative affairs and played a major role in the 1976 and 1980 Presidential campaigns. MacGregor had become senior vice-president, in Washington, of United Technologies. "Those are pretty heavy guys," Atwater said. "They coordinate."

6

From time to time in 1982, about ten people were gathered by
William Timmons and Clark MacGregor to breakfast at the University Club, in downtown Washington, near the offices of the
law firms and trade associations and corporate representatives,
to discuss how the various segments of American industry
could channel money into selected House and Senate races.
Then each of these people acted as host at a breakfast for a
particular industry group—pharmaceuticals, aerospace, transportation, and so on. One group was made up of lawyers and
consultants. Timmons himself served as the host of an event for
what he described to me as "a general business group."
Timmons & Company is one of the largest and most prosperous
of the Washington lobbying companies, with clients of the mag-
nitude of the Northrop Corporation, the G. D. Searle drug company, Chrysler, H. J. Heinz, Standard Oil of Indiana, Anheuser-
Busch, Eastern Air Lines, and Middle South Utilities. It also
does work for the Association of Trial Lawyers of America and
the National Rifle Association. Such a clientele gives Timmons
ready access to large amounts of money to help candidates. The
firm is essentially Republican, but—like all the major lobbying
firms in Washington which are dominated by people with ties
to one party—it maintains a smattering of members who have
connections with the other party. (Timmons hired an aide to
former House Speaker Carl Albert and a former lobbyist for the
United Auto Workers.) The people whom Timmons and Mac-
Gregor and their colleagues brought together were, essentially,

corporate representatives based in Washington—vice-presidents for corporate affairs, vice-presidents for public affairs, directors of a Washington office—and presidents or executive directors of trade associations. The corporate officers, Timmons says, do not run their company PACs, "but obviously they'll be listened to, or even asked, 'Who should we divvy up our goodies to?'" Corporate PACs are usually run at company headquarters. But an important part of the Washington representative's role is to help them make wise investments.

Of the breakfasts for industry groups, Timmons said, "We'd bring in twenty or so people who have some access to their industry or company PACs." Also in attendance were representatives of the Republican National Committee and the Party's Senate and House campaign committees—and Atwater. Timmons told me, "They describe the candidate and say, 'We think this is a good bet. He's ten points behind, but he was thirty points behind and is closing fast. If you want this kind of guy, he would be a good bet.' The purpose is to expose people who have access to PACs to what we think are good races." Each member of the Timmons-MacGregor group also held fund-raisers for particular candidates. "We got the room, bought the booze, drew up the invitation list to get some big names—a Cabinet officer, or Bush—to be there, and squeezed the arms," Timmons said. "To get people to come to a thousand-dollar-a-pop event is difficult. They may have already given a thousand, and you tell them, 'You've got to come up with another thousand—this guy has a real chance.' Some people don't like to see me on the street these days." Rick Shelby stayed in contact with the Timmons-MacGregor group down to the end, when the Republicans were particularly anxious to stem their losses, and the combined efforts of all concerned staved off disaster.

Other mechanisms also exist for the purpose of steering PAC money. According to both Atwater and Timmons, the Business-Industry Political Action Committee, BIPAC, also plays a significant role in coordinating the investment of business money in political campaigns. Bond says that BIPAC is "very important from a leadership perspective" because "it can send a very positive or negative signal through a potent group of PACS in any given campaign." BIPAC, which works with the White House on issues important to industry, has a number of large industries as members. It makes some campaign donations itself—in 1982, it contributed a total of two hundred thousand dollars to a hundred and forty-five candidates—but, more important, it recommends to its members which races to back. This gives BIPAC considerable influence, and candidates routinely visit its office, in Washington, seeking its endorsement. They also send it "PAC kits"—a new form of political literature, in which a candidate seeks to demonstrate why he would be a good investment. BIPAC was, in fact, begun in response to labor's activity by five directors of the National Association of Manufacturers. BIPAC has always been a bit mysterious about its origins, but an N.A.M. spokesman says his organization takes great pride in having formed BIPAC. The N.A.M. also puts out a newsletter called The PAC Manager, which indicates good political investments. Timmons told me, "A lot of candidates will make pilgrimages to talk to the people at BIPAC, because they represent heavy industry."

BIPAC will not give out a list of its members, but its chairman is the head of Armstrong World Industries, which manufactures floor and ceiling tiles and carpeting, and among its regional vice-chairmen are the heads of two large corporations noted for their involvement in conservative politics: J. Robert Fluor, the head of the Fluor Corporation, which is an international engineering and construction company; and Richard DeVos, president of the Amway Corporation, the second-largest direct-sales company in America. DeVos was the fourth-highest spender of independent funds for Reagan in 1980; the fifth-highest was Jay Van Andel, the chairman of Amway. DeVos was also finance chairman of the Republican National Committee from the spring of 1981 until the summer of 1982. In June of 1982, he was quoted in the press as saying, "This recession has been a beneficial thing and cleansing thing for this society." A spokesman for the R.N.C. says that DeVos resigned because of "a difference of styles."

Bernadette Budde, BIPAC's director of political education, wrote in 1979, "Candidates court us to a greater degree than ever." Miss Budde, a petite redhead, told me in September of 1982, "What happened is our market grew. Since 1963, we've always done what we do now, but now we've formalized it more. In 1972, we started holding briefings about elections with representatives of trade associations and corporations. Then, starting in 1978, we had more people interested in our recommendations, and the pool of people we shared information with has grown." Miss Budde made it clear that the growth of business PACS is related to the growth of government regulation of business. She has written, "A clear pattern emerges when reviewing who does and who does not have a PAC—the more regulated an industry and the more obvious an industry is as a congressional target, the more likely it is to have a political-action committee within the associations or within the companies that make up that industry." She continued, "As the government moves closer and closer to partnership with an industry, the result of that liaison is a PAC, mothered by industry but unmistakably sired by government."

And as the "partnership" between government and industry grew, so did BIPAC's business. Miss Budde told me that a few years ago a handful of people would attend BIPAC's briefings about the status of various races. Now, she said, the briefings are held every month, and between a hundred and a hundred and twenty-five people turn up—about three-fourths of them people in the Washington offices of corporations and trade associations. The meetings are "strictly informational," she said. "There is no attempt to tell people where to give money." But BIPAC does let it be known which candidates it is supporting and which races seem most promising. BIPAC also trades information with kindred spirits, such as the Chamber of Commerce, the N.A.M., the National Association of Home Builders, the National Association of Realtors, the A.M.A., and, of course, the Republican Party campaign committees.

The significance of BIPAC's own contributions is that they are a signal to the rest of the business community. BIPAC sends out a memorandum every few weeks indicating which races it is helping, and recommending that its members follow suit. BIPAC makes a point of giving early—it began making contributions to the 1982 campaign in 1981. Miss Budde said, "We need to be in early, because we know that others will be waiting for our recommendation. It's not really that our money matters so much; it's our blessing. If we're in there, the race isn't hopeless. If someone knows New Jersey but not California, he can call us and ask who we recommend." She said, "We were the first to have understood the importance of giving a blessing to a national campaign on behalf of a candidate for Congress. Now the Chamber of Commerce does it—it has a list of 'Opportunity Races.' It's not giving money, it's saying, 'These are people who meet our criteria.' "

BIPAC is considered a good source of information for what most PAC directors want to know: whom to bet on. Miss Budde said that, for example, people interested in the Clean Air Act from the point of view of business, assuming that the Act would not be revised before the end of 1982, called BIPAC. "They want to know which members of the Energy and Commerce Committee are going to return." The House Committee on Energy and Commerce has jurisdiction over the Act. Miss Budde said that some of BIPAC's contributions come from people whose companies don't have PACs; some come from companies whose treasuries are too small to enable them to have a political impact; and some come from companies with large PACs which have given the full amount to a candidate and give to BIPAC as "a way to supplement and extend" their contributions. BIPAC also offers a refuge for those with imperfect foresight. As Miss Budde put it, "If someone they didn't support wins, and we did support him, they can say that they gave to BIPAC."

When asked about the results BIPAC has achieved, Miss Budde

says, "It's changed the faces of a lot of members of Congress. Beyond that, a congressman who was out of touch with his community now hears voices he didn't hear before. If he had never heard from the doctors before, or had never heard from the car dealers before, he might have made different decisions, because he was operating in a vacuum." For these reasons, Miss Budde feels that BIPAC's impact has been to help create a more conservative Congress. "But," she adds, "we of the business community are very upset about the charge that members of Congress sell their votes. We of the business community have a very high regard for members of Congress. We're appalled by that sort of talk."

The one question that BIPAC lobbies on directly, Miss Budde says, is the issue of the campaign-spending laws: it wants an increase in the amounts that individuals are allowed to contribute, and some relief of the restrictions on how corporations raise PAC money. She is defiantly against any proposals to place a ceiling on the total amount that candidates can accept from political-action committees—a proposal that has gained increasing support in recent years—and is against public financing of congressional elections. According to David Obey, who, with Tom Railsback, Republican of Illinois, co-sponsored the 1979 bill to limit to seventy thousand dollars the total amount that a House candidate could receive from political-action committees, Miss Budde warned Capitol Hill aides that if their bosses voted for the Obey-Railsback bill they should not expect help from BIPAC. In addition, Obey says, a number of Republicans were told by representatives of various PACs around Washington that if they voted for the Obey-Railsback bill they would not receive much PAC money. At the end of 1982, BIPAC and like-minded organizations were gearing up for what they knew would be a big, long fight in Congress over further moves to change the campaign-finance laws.

BIPAC, then, has been a leader in the nationalization of political campaigns in its modern form: organizing contributions from outside a state or a congressional district. Miss Budde says with satisfaction that BIPAC was the first political-action commit-tee from outside Iowa to contribute to the House campaign of Tom Tauke, who defeated a Democratic incumbent there in 1978. The nationalization of campaigns by the big interest groups is a development that disturbs Jim Leach, a Republican representative from, as it happens, Iowa. Leach, who supports a limit on the amount of total PAC money a candidate can receive and also supports public financing of congressional campaigns, told me, "The state of Iowa is a classic example of the problem. We're mainly rural and small business, but in elections the Republicans are largely funded by business, much of which has nothing to do with the state, and the Democrats are funded by labor, much of which doesn't have anything to do with the state. And you see a breakdown in citizen access. Not that a constitu-ent isn't going to get in the door, but the guy who gave the money is going to get in first. So what you really see is a break-down in constitutional democracy, which is supposed to be based on citizen access and constituency access. We're seeing regional politics and state and citizen politics become national. National groups determine outcomes, whereas local constituen-cies used to provide the crucial role. This is new."

Inevitably, trade associations for PACs have grown up, some-times spawned by the PACs themselves, sometimes by enterpris-ing souls spotting an opportunity. One organization, called the National Association for Association Political Action Commit-tees, or NAFAPAC, was formed in 1980 to share information among trade- and professional-association PACs, and to fight what it sees as discrimination in the federal election laws against trade-association, as opposed to corporate, PACs. The issue has to do with rules that were designed to prevent business PACs from soliciting their own executives for their own PACs, and then, as part of a trade association, or several trade associations, solicit-ing them again. Also, NAFAPAC officials say they want the trade associations to get more attention from the politicians. Given the homage that is paid the trade associations—which have some of the largest PACs—it is difficult to understand what they are worried about, but all PACs want to be taken as seriously as possible by the practicing politicians, in order to get their money's worth. Richard Thaxton, vice-president of the political-affairs division of the National Association of Realtors (the highest-spending of all the business PACs and trade associations) and also the chairman of the board of NAFAPAC, said to me, "The media refers to corporate PACs and the amount they raise as if that's the measure of business giving, but the associations give more totally than corporations do. Yet the whole focus is on the corporations, and one of the problems on the Hill is that what the press writes, the public believes, and I'm not sure the association PACs are getting their proper shake."

Actually, trade associations, including groups with individual members, such as the auto dealers and the Realtors, and the Direct Selling Association, which is a member of NAFAPAC (direct sellers include such companies as Amway, Avon Products, and Mary Kay Cosmetics), have done very well legislatively. And they certainly have the politicians' attention. In June of 1982, NAFAPAC had a reception on Capitol Hill—"one of those cheapies, with wine and cheese," says J. Robert Brouse, the president of NAFAPAC—and over a hundred members of the House and Senate took the trouble to stop by. "They outnumbered our group three to one," Brouse says.

There is also something called the National Association of Business Political Action Committees, or NABPAC, a trade association of business PACs. It advises its two hundred and twenty-five member PACs on everything from PAC techniques and regulations to evaluations of candidates. Among its members are many of the largest corporations in America. Its literature uses the slogan "Democracy is not a spectator sport."

Both the Democratic and Republican party campaign organizations—the national committees, the Senate and House campaign committees—try to steer PAC money to their candidates. Both parties send out to likely PAC contributors newsletters touting their candidates; both hold meetings with friendly interest groups; both introduce new candidates to what is known in

[35]

Washington as "the PAC community." The Democrats, of course, receive substantial help from labor, in terms both of funds and of getting out the vote. Without the direct contributions from labor in 1982, many Democratic candidates, not to mention the Democratic Party itself, would have been in serious trouble. COPE contributed nearly nine hundred thousand dollars in members' voluntary contributions to the 1982 races, and PACS controlled by the A.F.L.-C.I.O. unions spent a little over one million dollars. And the A.F.L.-C.I.O. also expected to spend $3.5 million in union dues, through COPE, for voter registration and get-out-the-vote drives. COPE, under new management for this election, was deemed by Democratic officials to have become far more sophisticated and effective than in the past. In a way, it had to, because its effectiveness in the past was not impressive. Moreover, in 1982 it had something to rally around—unemployment.

Although no one can say exactly how much difference labor's get-out-the-vote drives made, Democratic officials say that labor activities were especially valuable in 1982 in the industrial states. The efforts of some unions—in particular the Communications Workers of America and the National Education Association, both of which are effective at getting out the vote—are considered more valuable than those of others. The United Auto Workers and the United Steelworkers, having watched their members defect to Reagan in 1980, worked hard, and successfully, to return them to the Democrats two years later. The N.E.A., which is not a member of the A.F.L.-C.I.O., spent about $1.4 million in the 1982 elections. Again Reagan handed the opposition some issues, in this case the level of funding for education, and such things as tuition tax credits and prayer in the schools, which the N.E.A. opposes. The N.E.A. had already headed off Reagan's promised abolition of the Department of Education. Says one N.E.A. strategist, "We got the issue pushed over into the election year, on the theory that members of Congress in close races wouldn't want to touch the issue. And we let Republicans know that anytime they took a shot at it, it would be an expensive shot." The other two most significant allies of the Democrats in 1982 were the environmentalists and the supporters of the nuclear-freeze movement. Again, the actions of the Reagan Administration helped galvanize these groups. The environmental groups, having been in business longer, could contribute more. Their contribution lay less in money than in volunteers who motivated the voters—with the unwitting help of James Watt, the Secretary of the Interior. The environmental movement, like the labor effort, was not solidly Democratic, however. Both business and labor, each for its own reason, tend to exaggerate labor's effectiveness. Recently, the Chamber of Commerce has begun get-out-the-vote drives (and businesses are allowed to spend to get their own employees to the polls), and the Republican Party, of course, spends large sums to get out its voters. So comparisons are impossible to make.

7

Starting in 1981, the Democrats, nearly desperate about the widening gap between the amounts of money the two parties can raise and alarmed by the growth of the business political-action committees and their willingness to finance challengers to Democratic incumbents, set out in systematic fashion to raise more business money themselves. They decided, says one House Democrat, to "fight fire with fire." The exercise had some unusual results. One result was the famous "bidding war" between the House Democrats and the White House over the Reagan Administration's 1981 proposal to cut taxes for individuals and businesses. The Democratic Party had only a technical majority in the House, and had to struggle for the votes of many of its Southern members, or "boll weevils." The bidding war was a result of the Democrats' desire not just to get their version of the tax bill passed, by offering special tax breaks in order to win votes on the House floor, but also to raise money from the interest groups that stood to benefit. Similarly, the fact that the House Ways and Means Committee avoided "marking up"—that is, drafting its own version of—the 1982 bill to raise taxes to close some of the enormous budget deficit caused by the 1981 bill, had to do with the Democrats' reluctance to offend certain interests. Charles Manatt, the Democratic National Committee chairman, and Byron Radaker, the chairman of the Party's Business Council, who is also the chairman and chief executive officer of the Congoleum Corporation, which manufactures floor coverings and is a major shipbuilder, sent a letter to every

Democratic member of Congress urging him not to vote for repeal of a provision that had become the symbol of the excesses of the 1981 tax cuts—the "safe harbor" provision, which allowed corporations to buy and sell tax deductions and credits. The letter, needless to say, caused a bit of an uproar within the Party.

Even the House Democrats' position paper, issued in September, 1982, setting out an agenda for the future was written with an eye on sources of business funds. Some of the Democrats who were involved in these exercises say that one of their motives is to try to prevent the Party from becoming the captive of labor: to prevent a final, absolute division of the American political system into a labor party and a business party. Their concern has presented some good opportunities to certain business interests.

In the days when the Texans Sam Rayburn and Lyndon Johnson and the Oklahoman Robert Kerr held power on Capitol Hill, Democrats enjoyed the blessings, and the contributions, of independent oil, and independent oil enjoyed the protection—in the form of generous tax breaks—of the Democratic Party. Moreover, there had been a kind of empathy between the independent-oil men and the Democrats: the independents were outsiders, often in conflict with the major oil companies, which, like other large corporations, were essentially Republican. Besides, in those days there simply weren't many Republicans from the South for independent oil to deal with. But after the election of a reform-minded Congress in 1974, and its reduction the following year of one of independent oil's most prized tax breaks, the depletion allowance, things began to change.

Until then, according to one oil lobbyist, independent oil was sixty percent Democratic. Then, in 1976, Jimmy Carter, in his effort to obtain the Democratic nomination, sought votes and money from the Southwest by promising to deregulate natural gas and by cultivating David Boren, who was then governor of Oklahoma and is now a senator, and getting his endorsement. Boren was the first governor to endorse Carter, and his doing so (even while Senator Lloyd Bentsen, a Texan and a key defender of the interests of independent oil, was still in the race for the Presidential nomination) helped Carter obtain independent-oil money. The oil industry had been trying for a long time to get natural gas deregulated. Shortly before the final election, Carter wrote a letter to Boren promising to push for deregulation of natural gas. (Actually, Boren himself wrote the letter. Boren, Robert Strauss, then the chairman of the Democratic National Committee, and Dolph Briscoe, then governor of Texas, thought up the letter at the Texas-Oklahoma football game at the Cotton Bowl, in Dallas, in October.) But after Carter was elected he changed his mind.

As it happens, the oil industry did fairly well under Carter—although he did not deregulate natural gas, he did increase the price of both gas and oil. Still, damaging as his about-face was, matters were made worse by the fact that early in his Administration, in pushing his energy legislation, he started talking about the "greed" of the oil companies. "People in Oklahoma felt they had been taken," Boren says. "That showed up in the 1980 elections." The oil industry got angrier and angrier—"They didn't think they were greedy," says an oil lobbyist—and, having been cultivated by the Republicans, felt that the best way to handle the situation was to go over to the other side. In the 1980 elections, independent-oil money reached the Republicans in unprecedented amounts. A Washington attorney for oil interests, Edward Forgotson, was among the few people who had the notion—a seemingly quixotic one at the time—that if the Republicans had enough money they could take over the Senate, and he decided to work to get oil money to Republican candidates for the Senate. Forgotson talked to the independent-oil PACs that had been springing up in the Southwest. (He also talked, he says, to General Motors and other corporations. Forgotson did such a good job that in 1981 and 1982 he served in an unpaid capacity as PAC director for the National Republican Senatorial Committee, and in 1981 he was also the PAC chairman for the Senate-House Republican fund-raising dinner.) And so in 1980 the oil money came in from Dallas, Houston, Midland, and Tulsa in both PAC money and individual contributions (most of it in the latter form), to help the Republicans in their attempts to unseat Democratic senators. Oil money was also an important factor in some attempts to unseat House Democrats. By then, according to the oil lobbyist, independent-oil money was ninety-five percent Republican.

The Democrats didn't like this turn of events at all. Early in 1981, Richard Kline, a Democrat and a lobbyist for a group of large independent oil producers in Texas, Oklahoma, Kansas, and Colorado, went to Representatives Tony Coelho, Democrat of California and the new chairman of the Democratic Congressional Campaign Committee, and Dan Rostenkowski, Democrat of Illinois and the new chairman of the House Ways and Means Committee. "The point I made to Tony and Danny," says Kline, "was let's get some of it back." So he proposed that the 1981 tax-cut bill include benefits for independent oil which could be paid for not by the taxpayers but by the major oil companies. Rostenkowski came to the conclusion that if the votes of enough "boll weevils"—Southern and Southwestern Democrats who had supported Reagan—could be guaranteed to get the bill passed he would go along. Rostenkowski's interest was less in raising money for the Democratic Party than in winning the fight with the Administration over the tax-cut bill. The Administration had already defeated James Jones, Democrat of Oklahoma and chairman of the Budget Committee, in the first big fight of 1981 (over the resolution establishing the outlines of the federal budget), and Rostenkowski wanted to do better. Out of such concerns come national policies.

Rostenkowski told Charles Wilson, Democrat of Texas, that he would make the deal if Wilson got commitments from six "boll weevils" to vote for the bill. Wilson, Richard Gephardt, a Democrat from St. Louis and a member of the Ways and Means Committee, and Gillis Long, Democrat of Louisiana and chairman of the House Democratic Caucus, were the leaders in the effort to put the deal together. Gephardt, who was first elected to Congress in 1976, at the age of thirty-five, was soon spotted by Kline, among others, as one of the House's "comers." (Kline, like some other lobbyists who do not have access to enormous amounts of money, prefers to concentrate on a few people who are particularly influential with their colleagues. This is simply another form of investing.) Kline needed someone who was not from an oil-producing state to try to persuade the House Democrats to go along with his scheme. He went to Gephardt to carry the argument after James Shannon, a thirty-year-old Democrat from Massachusetts and another influential member of the Ways and Means Committee, turned him down. Gephardt, a pleasant man with strawberry-blond hair, is one of the cool young politicians bred of the television age of politics. He is one of the new generation of Democrats—the "Atari Democrats"—who are trying to orient the party toward the world of "high tech," and is one of the most influential members of his generation in the House. He has worked closely with Coelho to try to broaden the financial base of the Democratic Party. Gephardt tried to get the support of thirteen or fourteen Southern Democrats, and eventually he and Wilson got what they took to be a firm commitment from the requisite six: Rostenkowski put some provisions for independent oil in the bill (but at less cost to the major producers).

But in the end the White House outbid the Democrats for the independent-oil votes, and the House passed the Administration-backed tax-cut bill, which contained a substantial tax break for independent oil producers. Only four "boll weevils" supported Rostenkowski's bill. So the Democrats' expensive strategy failed. But although the Democrats may not have prevailed on the tax bill, Kline and the other independent-oil interests came out ahead, because the year had begun with little prospect that anything at all would be done for independent oil.

The industry's vogue stemmed less from a careful consideration of what it could contribute to energy policy than from an awareness of what it could contribute to politicians—and its demonstrated willingness to try to unseat Democratic incumbents. Kline says, "I did everything I could after last year to raise money for Tony. I spent three weeks on the road. I raised eighty thousand dollars for the House Democratic campaign committee itself; that's not a lot, but it is a lot compared to what other industries have been giving them." Kline has also helped Senator Alan Cranston, Democrat of California, the main Senate money raiser for Democratic Senate campaigns. According to people Kline has talked to about this, he said to the oil people, "You're a geographical minority. You're just like black people— you're discriminated against because you're a minority. You have to be bipartisan." Then he told them something they were also being told by Robert Strauss, now an attorney in Washington and an energetic fund raiser. Strauss, too, had decided to help Coelho. Kline told them, "We could end up with a dangerous situation in this country—where business is one party and labor is the other." This is the same idea that was being expressed by some House Democrats, of course, and it serves the purposes of both. Kline also made a simple practical point to his oil audiences. He pointed out that "elections can turn on extraneous events—Watergate, Iran—so if the Democrats get control because of that kind of event we're going to get wiped out. So you have a stake in both parties." He told them that the Democrats had changed—that "it isn't the 1974 Party, because if it hadn't been for them there wouldn't have been a bidding war."

When the cost of the 1981 tax-cut bill forced Congress, starting with Republicans in the Senate, to raise taxes in 1982, the tax breaks that had been won the year before by independent oil were an obvious target. The Senate Finance Committee, headed by Robert Dole, Republican of Kansas, who is a defender of independent oil, declined to do anything to hurt independent oil. The committee had six Republicans up for reelection in 1982. Independent oil was in fact the one industry specifically exempted from the bill's cutback in corporate tax preferences. Kline was as eager as anyone that the House Ways and Means Committee not mark up the tax bill but instead send it straight to conference with the Senate—a most unusual procedure. Under the Constitution, tax legislation is supposed to originate in the House. It is generally understood that oil does better in the Senate than it does in the House, because the House has a larger ratio of members from non-oil-producing states. Rostenkowski and Barber Conable, Republican of New York and the ranking minority member of the Ways and Means Committee, worked up a list of proposals for tax reform which, among other things, would have removed a benefit that had been granted to independent oil the year before. The draft bill has been described by one House Democrat as "probably the greatest tax-reform package Congress would have ever passed."

But when the Democratic members of the Ways and Means Committee caucused to discuss these proposals, on the night of July 27th, Gephardt argued against the Democrats' writing their own tax bill, on the grounds that such a bill would inevitably divide the Democratic Party and that it was unlikely to pass. This, he said, would simply expose the Democrats to the charge of having caused a stalemate on the tax bill. As it happens, Coelho was also opposed to a Democratic markup of the bill, for the same reasons. Beryl Anthony, Democrat of Arkansas, argued that the oil provisions should not be included in the tax bill, because the Congressional Campaign Committee had been raising money from independent oil producers and had told them that they would be left alone. Another House Democrat had taken James Shannon aside on the House floor that day and made the same argument.

According to witnesses, after Anthony made that argument in caucus Shannon exploded. He said he was offended that Anthony would imply that the Democrats' votes were for sale. He then told the caucus about a meeting that had taken place in his office that afternoon: A young Washington lawyer, who had been a member of the Carter Administration, had come into his office and said that he had "a little technical provision" he wanted added to the tax bill (most lobbyists describe tax breaks for their clients as "a little technical provision"), and that his client was a good Democrat who had given a lot of money to the Party. Shannon had told the young lawyer, "I don't think you should be coming into our offices and telling us we should vote for something because anyone was giving us money." The lawyer, he continued, replied that in previous years, when he himself had worked on the Hill, such a thing would not have occurred. And then, Shannon told his colleagues, "he said to me, 'It's you guys who've caused this problem.' He said, 'I don't like doing this—it's terrible. But it's you guys who've put Congress on the auction block.' " Shannon also told the committee Democrats, "We have an economic crisis. We have to raise taxes, and we shouldn't be making judgments on the basis of who's giving campaign contributions." He said, "This is a tax-writing committee, not a fund-raising committee." Thomas Downey, a thirty-three-year-old Democrat from New York, backed Shannon. Downey told the caucus that the reality was that independent oil wasn't giving the Democrats anywhere near the amount of money that it had given the Republicans. Besides, Downey said, "we shouldn't be talking about this." In the end, the Democrats decided not to write a tax bill in the Ways and Means Committee. In the parlance of the time, they decided "not to put their fingerprints on it" in an election year.

The eagerness for independent-oil money is not, of course, limited to Democrats in the House. In 1982, a campaign consultant who was preparing television spots for a liberal Democratic senator running for reelection in a state where no oil is produced prepared one that attacked his opponent for taking money from oil interests. To the astonishment of the campaign consultant, he was asked to hold off running the spot. Eventually, the ad was run, but the hesitation was a symptom of the extent of the Democrats' anxiety. One Democratic senator, who declines to be quoted by name, says, "I've heard suggestions being made here differentiating between the big guys and the independents. The rationale for seeking out the independents is 'They're our kind of guys—they're not Texaco, Mobil, et cetera.' It's a tantalizing suggestion, because they say we're small people, they're small people. But personally I find it difficult to differentiate between them. They have differences among themselves, but in the end they're after the same thing."

Some other provisions of the 1981 tax-cut bill were also products of the Democrats' need to raise money. One was the provision that allowed people to buy tax-exempt "All-Savers Certificates." The proposal was cooked up by the troubled savings-and-loan industry, represented by the League of Savings Institutions, and was a major item in the bidding war. It was roundly criticized as one that would cost the Treasury nearly four billion dollars and would simply help the wealthy. But the savings-and-loan industry is known for its history of giving, and the Democrats, who used to be on the receiving end, wished to reinstate themselves. The history of this relationship somewhat resembles the one involving independent oil. Like the major oil companies, the bankers were Republicans, so the savings-and-loan institutions originally went to the opposition. And, according to Coelho, the parallel continues, in that, as the savings-and-loan business became more wealthy, it "went Republican." Coelho says, "All-Savers was a way to help the savings-and-loan industry. I appealed to them by saying that they had to help keep us alive." Coelho says that Gephardt was particularly instrumental in getting the All-Savers proposal through the House. Gephardt says that this had nothing to do with trying to raise campaign money. He says, "All-Savers was something to get the savings-and-loan business through the night." The proposal went through Congress with ease. Yet the All-Savers plan was such a failure that Congress refused to even entertain the idea of renewing it this year.

Another result of the bidding war, and of the Democrats' need for funds, was an item in the 1981 tax-cut bill which allowed corporate executives to get more favorable tax treatment of compensation provided in the form of stock options. In exchange, the corporations themselves lost their tax deductions for this compensation. This, then, was not so much a matter between the corporations and the Treasury as it was between the execu-

[46]

tives and the stockholders, who may or may not have been aware of it. One group that was interested in receiving such a favorable break was the new high-technology companies, which argued that this would be an effective way of compensating, and holding on to, their executives and scientists. Several Democrats look upon the new high-tech industry as a new source of funds. Major Washington law firms representing other corporations also lobbied for the provision—unbeknown, undoubtedly, to the corporations' stockholders.

Another very interested party was Steven Ross, the chairman of Warner Communications. In 1980, Ross, a major fund raiser for the Democratic Party, had threatened Carter Administration officials that he would not raise any more money for Carter unless the Administration supported the change. The Carter White House turned him down—both because the Treasury Department was opposed on the merits of the issue and because some White House aides told others that the threat was a blatant quid pro quo. One aide argued that it constituted a bribe. Another argument made within the White House was that word of such a deal was likely to leak to the press. (Often when people in government are trying to kill something, they base the argument not only on the merits but also on the fact that the press might find out about it.) Ross, whose company's stock had risen dramatically in recent years, was particularly eager that the provision be made retroactive. According to *Forbes* magazine, Ross in 1981 had the highest total compensation of any corporate executive in America—more than twenty-two million dollars, about twenty million of which was derived from stock options. In 1981, Ross gave generously to congressional Democrats well situated to be helpful to him. (Warner Communications, which has a number of legislative interests before Congress, also made substantial contributions in the 1981–82 period.) In 1981, the provision passed.

During the time that the Ways and Means Committee was considering the tax-cut bill, at least eleven of twenty-two Democrats on the committee who were planning to run for reelection held fund-raisers in Washington. (One Democrat, Ken Holland, of South Carolina, held a fund-raiser in March, 1981, and another a year later, and then announced that he was retiring from Congress.) The offices of two other Democrats declined to respond to queries about this. The fund-raisers were held from March through July of 1981—quite a long time before the November, 1982, elections. The word in the Washington lobbying community was that the fund-raisers were the congressmen's way of letting it be known that they were open for business. Even if, to be charitable, this was a cynical interpretation, it does suggest the problem: that congressmen, desperate for funds, had to raise money over the full two years of their term, and, while they were writing a tax bill, allowed themselves to be seen asking for funds from people seeking to influence the substance of that bill.

Tony Coelho's aggressive search for funds for the Party left mixed feelings among his colleagues. Coelho, forty years old, and slim, dark-eyed, and energetic, represents the Fresno area. While he protects the interests of the growers of his region, and there are some oil producers in his district, his politics have generally been liberal. Coelho says that he has been trying to regain the support of independent oil, and also to raise more money from Jews who support Israel—money that he has watched move from being fairly solidly Democratic toward the Republican Party. He attributes this to the fact that over half the House members had been elected for the first time within the past six years, when there had been a concern for a steady supply of foreign oil, and to Carter's having been more "objective" concerning the Arabs and Israel, and having backed the sale of F-15s to Saudi Arabia. Coelho says he has gone from meeting to meeting arguing that the two issues are interrelated—that a strong domestic oil industry will relieve pressure on Israel. He says that while he has not been "overwhelmingly" successful, he has raised more money—six million dollars—than any of his predecessors.

One area in which Coelho has, as he puts it, "scored the

greatest gains" is in persuading some of the biggest names in Democratic fund-raising to contribute to the House campaign committee. Previously, these people were for the most part interested only in Presidential and Senate races. Among the conquests Coelho listed were S. Lee Kling, a St. Louis banker who was formerly the finance chairman of the Democratic National Committee; Robert Strauss; Lew Wasserman, the chairman and chief executive officer of MCA; Walter Shorenstein, a San Francisco real-estate magnate; and John McMillian, the chairman of the Northwest Alaskan Pipeline Company. McMillian was the force behind getting Congress to approve an unprecedented policy of charging consumers in advance for the cost of building a natural-gas pipeline system, even if the project is never completed. The story, exposed by Bill Moyers on CBS, showed that McMillian had been a most generous contributor to the Democrats. Contributing to Coelho's committee and to individual House races is not, obviously, an entirely selfless act. Of course, some may do it because they philosophically favor Democrats. But many have another agenda as well.

Coelho followed one of the fashions in fund-raising by establishing a special club—this one called the Speaker's Club—for those who are especially generous: the admission charge is five thousand dollars a year for an individual and fifteen thousand dollars a year for a political-action committee. Cranston established a similar organization in the Senate, and both the House and the Senate Republican campaign committees have similar outfits, as do the Democratic and Republican National Committees. The idea is that the big givers are rewarded with meetings with important people. I asked Coelho what his club's members get, and he responded quickly and honestly, "Access. Access. That's the name of the game. They meet with the leadership and with the chairmen of the committees. We don't sell legislation; we sell the opportunity to be heard."

Gephardt explained to me his own concern for finding sources of funds for the Democratic Party. "If we assume the continuation of the world we're in, we have to broaden the base," he said. "The Democrats have been outspent and will continue to be outspent, but we can't be outspent by ten or twenty to one and survive. We have to get smaller donations from individuals in greater volume; we have to get donations from business in greater volume; and we have to get at the PACS, which are growing like crocuses in the spring." As for his efforts on behalf of independent oil, Gephardt said, "I felt it was not only good energy policy but also would allow us to show domestic drillers that we were not down on everything they were for—which was their impression. If you look at the 1980 campaign, you'll find incredible amounts of oil money going into Republican campaigns. The drillers had become increasingly Republican and aggressively Republican. I felt if we were going to try to hold our party together for the tax bill—to hold the 'boll weevils' and win—we had to do something about independent oil."

Gephardt was one of the principal authors of the economic paper that the House Democratic Caucus published, after much straining for agreement, in September of 1982. It strongly reflects the Atari Democrats' optimism about the possibilities of high technology for the economy, and it also reflects their interest in the industry as a source of funds. Gephardt said to me, "The whole economic paper is an attempt to say that Democrats are interested in growth—in the private sector and business growing and prospering—as well as in seeing that government is fair and trying to help people. In the nineteen-sixties and seventies, the Party came to be seen as interested only in redistribution of income and fairness; we assumed that there would be economic growth. That image has hurt the Party and our relationship with a broad spectrum, so we had to show that we are interested not only in redistribution and fairness but also in making the economy grow and having business prosper."

Though Gephardt himself is flourishing under the present system of campaign financing—the special interests are particularly eager to contribute to him, and he raised far more than he needed for his 1982 campaign, which he won by seventy-eight percent—he argues that the system should be changed. It was Gephardt who used the word "fever" to describe the money-raising atmosphere on Capitol Hill. He said, "If you have the need to raise three or four hundred thousand dollars, you're taking an enormous amount of the members' time just to raise the money. And, whether it's conclusive or not, it has to have an increasing impact on the legislative outcome. Part of it's psychological. A kind of fever takes over. Members hear that someone else is raising five hundred thousand dollars, and they think they have to raise five hundred thousand dollars, and soon everyone thinks he has to raise five hundred thousand dollars, and it's disruptive to the public process. We've got to construct a system of campaign financing so that a representative or a senator feels confident that his responsibility runs to the large public mass in his constituency, and he doesn't have any overwhelming tie to any group."

I asked Gephardt about the argument made by some that the Democrats were concerned about the campaign-financing system now only because business had become organized and was outspending labor.

He replied, "It shouldn't be possible for labor or management or environmentalists or anyone else to have this importance in the electoral process. That's not the way it should work."

James Shannon is among those who see a problem in the Democrats' scramble for money. He says, "The problem of money in politics hasn't been an obsession of mine, but it's becoming one now. We on the Democratic side came out of the 1980 election and saw we got clobbered, in large part because of money. So the whole subject has come out of the closet. There has been all too much discussion around here about how what we do in the House and on our committees is going to affect our ability to raise money. I mean, people aren't embarrassed about saying this anymore. I'm not a virgin on this; I take PAC money—that's part of the process. But what happened after 1980 was that a lot of special interests swooped down on the Democratic Party and said, 'Look, fellas, we're good Democrats, and we should play the same game the Republicans played, and we're going to show you how to do it.' I'm no Common Causer, but this stuff has really been bothering me." And he adds, "You go where the money is if you want to raise money, and it's not going to be with the traditional Democratic constituencies. That's the problem. That's what's feeding the ideological problem we've got."

That is a very big point. The problem the Democrats have had in defining themselves stems in some part—perhaps a substantial part—from their dilemma over where to turn for money. Shannon is a recent convert to the idea of public financing of congressional campaigns, and he says that his conversion came as a result of the maneuvering on the 1982 tax-increase bill. "The argument 'Let's not put our fingerprints on it'—that's something for the special interests to hide behind," he says. "What's bothering me is when you start seeing guys acting against what you know are their philosophies and constituencies and instincts. When you see non-oil-state people acting for oil interests, you have to ask why. We all talk a lot about taking contributions and saying no, but—what's that line?—after all is said and done, more is said than done. There are some here who say that PACs don't influence public policy. That's baloney. There's nothing wrong with advocating an interest that you think is worthy, that is going to benefit an industry or group, and then for that industry or group to give you political support. But the key is that the interest has to be worthy and the issue has to be worthy, and you have to be able to say no when the issue isn't worthy. And that's some of what I think is being lost around here." Says David Obey, "As the Democrats get more troubled about money, the Party gets leeched."

8

Just as the search for money caused divisions among the Democrats, it served as a unifying force among the Republicans. The Democrats are by nature a less cohesive group than the Republicans, but the factor of money reinforces each party's natural inclinations. At least for a time—until the pressures to stay with Reagan collided with the political realities of getting re-elected—the Republicans' access to money acted as a disciplining force. First, there is the simple fact that the Republican Party has recruited, groomed, and given substantial support to its candidates. Once the successful candidates have reached Washington, they have been cosseted and kept in touch with. They have been part of a group. Then, there are a number of other things that a White House with access to money, and the willingness to make use of that access, can do. One of President Reagan's top aides told me, "Now, when we have a vote coming up and the Realtors are supporting our position on that vote, the word can go out that it would be good if they would get their members to call members of Congress. We can't do it directly." The "indirect" methods used by the White House are clear-cut enough. "But we can let others know. The word gets around fast. The Chamber of Commerce can also be helpful. Then we can call Congressman So-and-So and say, 'This bill is important to the Realtors, and, remember, you got five thousand dollars from them.' " Lyn Nofziger, who was the Reagan White House political-affairs director in 1981 and then became a political consultant, says, "It's just a matter of calling them up or bringing them in and saying, 'This is important to the President and the country'—and just sending them out to go to work." The President's aide continued, "The best way for us to encourage discipline is for us to make it clear that the President is more likely to raise funds for you if you support him than if you do not." He added, "We're doing some fund-raisers in this campaign as a result of some votes."

Trent Lott, Republican of Mississippi and the House Republican Whip, told me that when a newly elected Republican congressman arrives in Washington "it helps that we can go to him and say, 'We were able to get you here and provide you money.' " He added, "And we can get grassroots groups that supported him to make themselves heard when there's a vote." He offered as examples the Realtors ("the best association I've seen in this city") and the National Federation of Independent Business—a powerful network of service-station owners, food-store owners, and the like. There were, of course, some votes in the 1982 session of Congress on which Republicans went against Reagan—in one important instance, the overriding of his veto of a supplemental appropriations bill—causing him to lose. Lott explained, "We're still a minority party. We can't get hung up on a litmus test when we're trying to build a majority." So if a Republican felt he had to break ranks in order to get reelected, the leadership understood. "In the last thirty days, we've let a lot of people go," Lott said to me in late September. "We know it's the political season. You don't break arms on a jobs bill. People are very nervous now." He told me, "We worked very, very closely on legislation with the various business, corporation, association, professional, and philosophical groups." Of course, these groups' efforts to help the Administration can also be of benefit to themselves, even though they may start out in philosophical agreement. One Republican official said that such groups—the Chamber of Commerce, BIPAC, the N.F.I.B., the Realtors, the National Association of Home Builders—have access to the Reagan White House through its political office, through the office that maintains liaison with outside interest groups, through the congressional-liaison office, and, most important perhaps, through a special task force working on reducing government regulations, headed by Vice-President Bush. "They call there all the time," one Administration aide says.

Rich Bond, of the R.N.C., was quoted in the *Wall Street Journal* in August of 1982 as saying that he had persuaded two Republicans to vote for the President's 1982 budget cuts. "I said, 'Look—what if I can guarantee we'll max out on you?' " ("Max out" in this context means giving a candidate the maximum amount a party can give in direct contributions. Individuals who have contributed all they can under the law are said to be "maxed out.") Bond also said, "We'll help you do a quick-and-dirty newsletter, make a commercial, organize a town meeting. Boom. Boom. Boom." If the two congressmen had not supported the President, Bond explained, "I would have nailed them to the wall."

The Republican Party's access to large amounts of money helped Reagan govern in other ways. The Party's bountiful treasury has enabled Richard Wirthlin, whose polling for the White House is paid for by the National Committee, to have the latest equipment in polling devices. With something called Computer Assisted Telephone Interviewing, or CATI, Wirthlin can gather more sophisticated information than ever before, and gather it more quickly. For example, the President gave a speech on the 1982 tax-increase bill on a Monday night; by Tuesday night Wirthlin's polling operation had detailed information on how the public had reacted; by Wednesday the Administration was able to deliver material to members of Congress telling them which arguments worked best with the public. In 1983, Wirthlin installed a still more sophisticated system. And the Republican National Committee took the concept of soft money to yet another frontier by using it to run thirty- and sixty-second spots, in those states that permit soft money, of the President delivering his tax speech. Actually, though the spots appeared to be excerpts of the President delivering his speech, they had been cut ahead of time.

As it turned out in November, 1982, Lott's—and the President's—troops had had cause to be nervous. And one result of the 1982 elections was to inject more independence into the Republican members of Congress. (Among other things, about eighteen of those Republicans who lost their House seats had been first-termers who were true loyalists. And many of the House and Senate Republicans who survived did so by separating themselves from the President's economic program.) But the moral of the story is not that an Administration and a party cannot use money effectively to enforce unity; the moral is that they can use it very effectively—but only up to a point. Faced with the choice between showing gratitude or surviving, most politicians do not have difficulty deciding.

9

The chase for political money has led to the institutionalization of the Washington fund-raiser: the ritual event—usually a cocktail party, but there are variations—at which a politician provides an opportunity for lobbyists and political-action committees to turn up and give him money. Often, the fund-raisers are staged by the lawyer-lobbyists themselves; sometimes they are staged by the candidate, with party luminaries acting as honorary hosts (or allowing their names to be put on the invitations). At the height of the political season, in the fall of an election year, there will be at least a dozen fund-raisers going on in Washington on any given weeknight. But in fact fund-raisers have now become a year-round phenomenon. The lawyer-lobbyists and the lobbyists for trade associations that like to spread their money around become exhausted racing about town to these gatherings. It is important to turn up in person.

Politicians who used to make it a point to raise most of their funds back home—they didn't want word to get back to their districts and states that they had taken any money from "Washington," and they didn't in those days need so much money to run—now find the Washington money pot hard to resist. When Mike Mansfield, the former Senate Majority Leader, was up for reelection in 1964, he simply wrote his Montana constituents that he was too busy with his Washington duties to come back to campaign, and he spent about a hundred and twenty thousand dollars for his reelection. In 1982, Senate Minority Leader Robert Byrd, Democrat of West Virginia, nearly wore himself to a frazzle raising money for his own reelection—and as of mid-October he had spent about $1.2 million. And it is not just candidates for the Senate and the House who have Washington fund-raisers held in their behalf. Candidates for governor and lieutenant governor also trek to Washington for money. There is even a firm in Washington that specializes in arranging fund-raising parties for Democrats.

One young Washington lawyer, whose practice is beginning to flourish, and who makes the fund-raising rounds himself, told me, "Ninety-nine percent of lobbying in this city is now fund-raising." He continued, "The standard price of going to a fund-raiser used to be a hundred dollars. Now it's two hundred and fifty dollars. For that, you get your standard cocktail party. The food's the same, the people are the same, the conversation is the same. For five hundred dollars, you get either a smaller group and better food or maybe a buffet dinner. For a thousand dollars, you get a sit-down dinner in a fancy house." There are a few Washington homes—the Averell Harrimans' among them—that are frequently put to use for fund-raisers.

I asked the young lawyer why he went to so many fund-raisers.

He replied, "If you're a friend of the congressman, or if you're doing a favor for a friend who calls you for money, you send a check. But there are reasons you might want to be seen to be there. If you want to see a couple of congressmen and staff members—people you want to do business with—you have a good chance of running into them. And if you want the congressman to know that you contributed, you don't want to count on his reading the list to see who gave." He added, "There's an elaborate system of getting the right people to make the calls to get people to go to a fund-raiser. The right person calling can get me to show up."

The role of the lobbyist–fund raiser has given prominence to a new style of lawyer in Washington. The older, more staid firms still do their lawyering and their lobbying (though some decline to call it that) and their fixing (even fewer would call it that), but the new razzle-dazzle lobbyist–fund raisers are now the most visible members of the cast. They raise money, which purchases them access, which impresses their clients, which enables them to raise more money, which enables them to get more clients, which enables them to purchase more access, and on it goes. The young lawyer said, with a mixture of admiration and envy, "They raise money from their clients. They just hit them up. The clients by and large have PACs. The PAC gets credit for it; the lawyer gets credit for it; everybody's happy." (Robert McCandless, one of this new crowd, has been quoted in the *Wall Street Journal* as saying that he would not accept a client who was not willing to set up a political-action committee.)

As a Capitol Hill aide explains it, "Those lawyers have a very sophisticated arbitrage arrangement. They come to a congressman and say, 'I know you have a tough campaign and need some money, and I'll throw you a party,' and they'll raise you ten thousand dollars." The aide was being conservative in his estimate. He went on, "If they raise ten thousand dollars, then they have access to you. Then they turn around and get more clients and represent their interests before Congress. Why? Because they can show them that they have access to people in Congress. So a ten-thousand-dollar fund-raiser is arbitraged into twenty or thirty thousand dollars in legal practice." The aide was being conservative in this case as well. Actually, no self-respecting money raiser wants to put on a fund-raiser that yields a mere ten thousand dollars. Thomas Boggs, one of the premiere lawyer-lobbyist money raisers in Washington, says, "We'd be embarrassed to have fund-raisers that end up with less than fifteen thousand dollars. If we raise thirty, forty thousand dollars or over, that's good." Boggs is forty-two, and has an innocent moon face, a low-key, pleasant manner, and an understanding of politics that would impress Machiavelli. In a sense, he was born to the role, being the son of the late Hale Boggs, Democrat of Louisiana, who was the House Majority Leader, and Corinne Boggs, who has represented her husband's district since he died in an airplane crash, in 1972. Over lunch one day,

Thomas Boggs explained to me the niceties of these occasions. "The Washington fund-raiser is not successful without PAC money," he said. "That is, not unless you have an unusual kind of race, about which a lot of individuals feel very strongly." Boggs maintained that the amount of money that comes out of a fund-raiser—thirty thousand dollars, say—is "a pittance" in a Senate race, which costs at least a million dollars.

Why, then, I asked him is the fund-raiser so important?

"Because you want to have a successful Washington event for someone," he replied. He went on to explain, "It has connotations for your relationship with the member. And it has connotations with constituency groups around the country. If a senator is showered with special-interest money in Washington, then the special interests in Chicago and Los Angeles and New York will follow suit. If they see he's a player in Washington, they want to play along. The fear factor is also very important. If the fund-raiser is a failure, it has repercussions, and those repercussions affect you. They also affect the candidate's ability to raise money."

I asked Boggs what he does to try to make a fund-raiser a success.

He replied, "Most of the smaller PACs are oriented to their own self-interest and basically reward members who have helped them. If a guy's on the Senate Banking Committee and he's supported Glass-Steagall, you go to the securities industry. If he's opposed it, you go to the banking industry." The Glass-Steagall Banking Act of 1933, which prohibited commercial banks from also being in the investment business, has pitted the banking industry against the securities industry for years. In 1982, there was an attempt in the Senate Banking Committee to change the law to allow banks to underwrite municipal bonds. The attempt failed. Boggs said, "A guy like me doesn't really care what side he was on if I'm raising money for him. If someone's on the Agriculture Committee and he's supported price supports for sugar, I'd go to the sugar producers—in Florida,

Louisiana, and Hawaii. If he voted against it, I'd go to the candy manufacturers."

Boggs' fund-raisers range from those he has held in his own offices ("It's cheap") to ones held at the Hyatt Regency Capitol Hill Hotel (a popular spot for fund-raisers), to a fine dinner for a group of congressmen at a good restaurant (the charge for that: a thousand dollars a head). Boggs will also arrange a small dinner for a politician he feels the PACs may have the wrong impression of—that is, they may feel he's too anti-business. Boggs also said there are some politicians you don't want to expose to the donors too much. Though Boggs has a few Republicans in his firm, his fund-raising efforts are, with one or two exceptions, limited to Democrats. Of course, if enough money raisers are going to stage enough successful fund-raisers, mutual assistance is required. Boggs says, "A lot of us scratch each other's backs. Sometimes I'm trying to raise money for someone nobody's ever heard of—someone who's running in a district where there's no incumbent—and I get money from two or three guys. They could be other lawyers, other lobbyists, or PAC representatives. I know damn well they're going to call me in two or three days for someone I've never heard of. You could almost put us on a recording and put it on the phone. We get pretty tired of each other."

One result of all these people raising money can be overlapping claims to the credit for raising it. An aide to one politician says, "Four different people will tell you that they will raise fifty thousand dollars for you, and you end up with seventy-seven thousand dollars, and wonder what happened to the other hundred and twenty-three. They're all claiming to have raised the same money, and they get into terrible fights about it."

The astute lawyer-lobbyist does not direct his efforts only toward those who need his help; he also puts his (and others') money on sure winners. For example, in July, 1982, J. D. Williams, one of the most notable lawyer-lobbyist money raisers in Washington, sent a letter to other lobbyists on behalf of Senator Howard Metzenbaum, Democrat of Ohio, who is one of the most liberal members of the Senate. Metzenbaum, Williams wrote, "is the overwhelming favorite in the Ohio Senate race." In other words, give to him *because* he is going to win. The letter, on Williams' stationery, was co-signed by eight others, including Boggs; Stuart Eizenstat, a former assistant to Jimmy Carter and now in private practice; Pat O'Connor, a lawyer and major Democratic fund raiser; Ned Gerrity, a senior vice-president of the International Telephone and Telegraph Corporation; Jack Valenti, president of the Motion Picture Association; and lobbyists for General Electric, the oil-and-gas industry, and the National Retail Merchants Association. Metzenbaum serves on the Judiciary Committee (which has major anti-trust and copyright issues before it), the Energy and Natural Resources Committee, the Budget Committee, and the Labor and Human Resources Committee. The letter said, "We are aware that, in some quarters, Howard Metzenbaum is charged with being 'anti-business.' We have had occasion to deal with him on many issues and we have found him to be a willing listener and helpful on several issues." The letter mentioned that Metzenbaum had supported the 1981 tax-cut bill and other tax breaks for business.

Williams, a forty-four-year-old Oklahoman who declines to give interviews, is, like Boggs, a Democrat, but he doesn't mind going where the exigencies of business propel him. During the 1982 deliberations over where to find the revenues to raise taxes, Williams was on the telephone to Robert Dole almost every morning, telling Dole that he could get him two or three votes for this or that proposal. Williams, of course, had some interests he wanted protected and, Dole was aware, had clients who might contribute to the political-action committee, Campaign America, that Dole himself had established, in preparation for a possible run for the Presidency in 1984. And House Democrats were surprised to hear White House aides praise Williams for being very helpful to them in getting the 1982 tax-increase bill through. As it happened, an item in the tax bill that was of major interest to Williams was the one involving safe-harbor tax leasing. A Williams client, General Electric, had done well under the tax-leasing system that existed before the 1981 tax-cut bill. The 1981 bill opened up tax leasing to new categories of business, and thus created competition in the market for tax deductions and credits. Moreover, the focus in the press on abuses under the safe-harbor law threatened companies, including G.E., that had been comfortably nestling there before the new rivals came along. Those representing the companies that benefitted from the 1981 change were trying to preserve what they could, and were willing to sacrifice G.E. Thus, Williams, representing G.E., was on the side of "reform"—that is, of repealing the 1981 provision, with the result that his client would be comfortably off once again. And so he made himself helpful to Dole and the White House.

The fight over safe-harbor leasing was one of the more spectacular examples of how the lawyer-lobbyists all get involved in an intricate quadrille, sometimes working together, sometimes opposing each other. Williams' friend Boggs represented Chrysler, which stood to benefit from the new law, so he was opposed to Williams on this issue. It may be remembered that Byron Radaker, the chairman of the Congoleum Corporation and also the chairman of the Democratic Business Council, had written, along with Party Chairman Charles Manatt, to every member of Congress asking that the new safe-harbor law be protected. Boggs told me that he had talked Radaker into taking the job as Business Council chairman. Radaker is also a client of Boggs'. Charls Walker, the business lobbyist, who was one of the champions of the safe-harbor-leasing provision of 1981, was in this instance on the same side as Boggs; in other instances they have been on opposite sides. In the case of safe-harbor leasing, they lost.

Robert Strauss also occupies a place in the pantheon of lawyer-lobbyist money raisers; in fact, it is unusual in the case of any hotly contested legislative issue not to find that one side or the other has signed up Strauss, Williams, or Boggs, as well as some others. Increasingly, the legislative fights have become struggles among the major lobbyists, all of them equipped with war chests. (It is not uncommon for interests with large stakes to take out insurance by signing up more than one lobbyist, in order to gain access to both sides of the street. Chrysler had signed up both Timmons and Boggs, as has the Association of Trial Lawyers of America.) Strauss, of course, has been raising money for Democrats in one capacity or another for years. He told me in September of 1982, "There hasn't been anybody who can reach the rich people the way I can." And he added, "Except maybe Lee Kling, who can reach Wall Street and financial circles." Strauss gives his own fund-raisers and circulates at others. Like his Democratic colleagues, he helps see to it that corporate money still flows to Democrats—particularly incumbents. "Those companies are hedging their bets," he said. Strauss helped educate Senate Minority Leader Byrd in the ways of national fund-raising. Byrd had never had to bother with such things before, but in 1981 he had been singled out by Republicans as a potentially vulnerable candidate, and there were threats of large amounts of money coming in against him. The National Conservative Political Action Committee, or NCPAC, had also listed him as a target. So, coached by Strauss and others, Byrd travelled around the country to the Democratic funding sources, and on the evening of the day I talked to Strauss there was to be a fund-raiser for Byrd at the Hyatt Regency in Washington. "You'd be surprised at the companies that will be there," Strauss said. Strauss and his friend Russell Long, the Democratic senator from Louisiana who has for years directed others' money to his colleagues, hit the road together to raise money for incumbent Democratic senators. Strauss told me, "I know a man in Houston who will give Russell Long or me money for almost any candidate if we describe him as a moderate or a conservative. They won't give to the party committees, because that money might go to 'those goddam left-wingers.' One man wants to know where a candidate stands on defense. Another wants to know where he stands on social issues. Another wants to know where he stands on the pipeline. They want to give to a man whose stand they know."

I asked Strauss what he does when a candidate calls and asks him to raise money for him.

He replied, "First, I take a look and see what committee he's on. Then I call a couple of friends in a couple of communities and I say, 'Senator So-and-So is on such-and-such a committee and he's interested in your problems. He's going to be in New York, and I think you'd like to see him.' The pattern is that a politician goes to the people in the field he handles—somebody involved in defense goes to the people in that industry—and those people usually do some work for him. They're not buying anything: he votes for them sometimes and against them sometimes. Then he goes to people who simply like to help Democrats. The next thing you do that's important is you go to a significant man or woman in a town—I'm talking about a Lew Wasserman or a Bob Strauss—and say, 'Would you do me a favor? I want you to host an affair.' People will come to the affair. He'll attract a hundred people. You don't ask them for money—just to come to the affair. Then the senator or congressman comes and makes his pitch, and then the politician or the host or his staff follows up with phone calls."

Strauss ticked off the names of the major Democratic money raisers in America, and said whether each followed up with calls or had staff people do so, or what. "I have that all right here," he said, pointing to his head. "Then, there's people like me, who have been in politics a long time and have an apparatus all across the country. People are constantly calling us for favors." Referring to his wise and able executive assistant, Vera Murray, Strauss said, "Vera knows these people. She can call any town in the country and she's got someone who can help." He continued, "Sometimes people would rather make a half-dozen phone calls than give an event. They call their family and social and business contacts. They can produce a few thousand dollars that way. They're relieved as hell they don't have to host a party. Sometimes I'll call a fellow and say, 'Look, Senator So-and-So needs money. You don't have to give a fund-raiser—just make a few calls. Give for yourself, your wife, your kids. Get a few of your friends to do the same thing.' "

At the time we talked, in September, Strauss said that he had probably given forty-five thousand dollars himself. Moreover, his law firm—Akin, Gump, Strauss, Hauer & Feld—maintains its own PAC, as do some other law firms in Washington. In 1981–82, Akin, Gump's PAC gave more than that of any other law firm (almost fifty-nine thousand dollars as of July, 1982). One of the more unexpected politicians—at least at first glance—for whom both Akin, Gump and Thomas Boggs raised money in 1982 was Representative Fortney Stark, Democrat of California, who is one of the most liberal members of the House. In a letter inviting other lawyers to have lunch with Stark and contribute five hundred dollars, an Akin, Gump partner pointed out that Stark, in September of 1981, had taken over a position that is of great interest to the lawyer-lobbyists: he had become chairman of the House Ways and Means Committee's Select Revenue Measures Subcommittee. That subcommittee is where a lobbyist turns if he is seeking enactment of a special tax provision. These are provisions that affect a particular client, and are the ones that are usually described by the lobbyist as "just a little technical amendment" that "won't cost the treasury much." In its time, the subcommittee has been referred to on Capitol Hill as "Santa's workshop."

10

Serving on some congressional committees is more lucrative—
the term is actually used on Capitol Hill—than it is on others,
the most lucrative being the House Ways and Means and Senate
Finance Committees, which have jurisdiction over tax legislation, and the House Energy and Commerce Committee and the
Senate Committee on Commerce, Science, and Transportation.
The Commerce Committees have jurisdiction over, among other
things, regulatory policy affecting business. By contrast, serving on the Judiciary Committees, whose purpose is to watch
over the Constitution and deal with the subject of crime, is not
nearly so financially rewarding. Only the subject of anti-trust,
which produced a major lobbying fight in the Ninety-seventh
Congress, began to make it more profitable to sit on Judiciary,
and only the infusion of ethnic money—Greek and Taiwanese
as well as Jewish and, increasingly, Arab—makes it financially
worthwhile at all to sit on the committees that monitor the
conduct of foreign policy. In 1980, the total PAC contributions to
members of the Ways and Means Committee and the House
Commerce Committee were roughly twice the total contributions to members of the Judiciary and Foreign Affairs Committees. (The PAC listings with the Federal Election Commission are
only partially revealing, of course, since people with interests
before Congress do not funnel all their contributions through
PACs.) A similar picture emerged from a study of the F.E.C. reports of PAC contributions as of late November, 1982. (Candidates
for federal office must file quarterly reports with the F.E.C. of all
contributions and expenditures. There would be little change

after November.) As of November, 1982, the House Energy and Commerce Committee members who ran for reelection to the House had been given a total of $3.6 million. House Ways and Means Committee members had been given $3.5 million. House Judiciary Committee members had received $1.7 million, and House Foreign Affairs Committee members had been given less than $2.5 million. Thus, it is worth far less to watch over foreign policy, and half as much to guard the Constitution, as it is to write tax laws and preside over regulatory and energy policy.

It is not uncommon for strategically placed congressmen who do not have real election challenges to be beneficiaries of PAC investments. For example, in 1980 Representative Ken Holland, Democrat of South Carolina and a member of the Ways and Means Committee, had no primary contest and won the general election with eighty-eight percent of the vote, yet he received more than seventy-three thousand dollars from PACs. Kent Hance, Democrat of Texas, who was appointed to Ways and Means in 1981 and was the co-author of the Administration-backed substitute for the committee's 1981 tax-cut bill, had no primary opposition in 1982 and won the general election with eighty-two percent of the vote; in 1982 he received nearly four hundred and fifty thousand dollars in total contributions. Some Republicans who barely glimpsed an opponent in 1980 were similarly remunerated. In 1982, twenty-four members of Congress who were unopposed in the general election and had either minor or no primary opposition received at least fifty thousand dollars from PACs. Eight of them received over a hundred thousand dollars in PAC money. The grand master of raising money that he doesn't need was Dan Rostenkowski. Rostenkowski, a product of Chicago's machine politics, hasn't had a real election challenge since he decided to go to Congress, in 1958. In 1980, he won with eighty-five percent of the vote and received a hundred and eighty thousand dollars in PAC money. In 1982, when Rostenkowski, who had now become the chairman of Ways and Means, was similarly worry-free—he won by eighty-four percent—he had four hundred and ninety-five thousand dollars on hand at the end of 1982. Rostenkowski explains that he needs the money "for a rainy day." (Rostenkowski did oppose the renomination of Jane Byrne, the mayor of Chicago, supporting instead Richard M. Daley, the son of the late mayor—an act that was not without political risk. As things turned out, both Byrne and Daley lost.) In October, 1981, Rostenkowski held his first Washington fund-raiser. Every lawyer-lobbyist in town felt he had to turn up. Rostenkowski said to me before the election, "If I'm anything in politics, I'm a learner. I know the best defense is an offense. Anyone who thinks of running against me knows two things: one, I get back to my district; two, I've got a fund. And if I had to raise a lot more, I could. That fund gives one a little bit of independence. I know people would say that fund means I'm bought. There's no relationship between that fund and my record. Bob Michel is suffering in a close race now—he doesn't have a fund." (Rostenkowski has been in the forefront of those who oppose public financing of campaigns.)

Rostenkowski, like a number of other House members, also puts his surplus funds to use to help his fellowman, and thereby help himself. Bill Frenzel, a Republican from Minnesota and a member of the Ways and Means Committee, has also been very active in dispensing campaign funds to his colleagues. One lawyer-lobbyist says that incumbents without real election challenges consider money from some of the larger political-action committees their "just due." Some House members accumulate large funds, which they carry over from election to election. Some store the money up for a run for the Senate. Some invest it. Some use campaign funds for questionable purposes: campaign funds are not supposed to be put to personal use, but some members are less than fastidious about this. Some use the funds for their offices, or for some things—meals, trips, and what-have-you—that it takes some imagination to call reelection activities.

Tom Boggs' father may have started the tradition of congressional leaders' maintaining funds from which they disburse contributions to their colleagues. O'Neill and Jim Wright, the House Majority Leader, and Gillis Long, the chairman of the House Democratic Caucus, have such funds. One reason some members maintain such funds is to help themselves in the House. Another reason is that they can act as a conduit for groups or individuals who have already given a particular candidate all they are allowed to under the law. One member of Congress says, "They buy power for themselves by spreading the money around." A notable example of such generosity occurred in 1979, when Representative Henry Waxman, Democrat of California, who was trying to win the chairmanship of the Health and the Environment Subcommittee of the House Commerce Committee, distributed about forty thousand dollars to thirty of his House colleagues, including eight who served on Commerce. Seven of the eight voted for Waxman, and he defeated Richardson Preyer, a respected representative from North Carolina, who according to seniority was in line for the job.

The honeylike attraction of members of the House Energy and Commerce Committee is apparent in their contributions reports. The list of fields over which the committee has jurisdiction indicates the nature and the size of the interests that would want to be in good standing with its members: oversight of most of the federal regulatory agencies; energy and power; health; environment; telecommunications; consumer protection; finance (meaning the securities industry and to some extent the commodities exchanges); fossil and synthetic fuels; transportation; commerce; and tourism. According to Common Cause, twenty-one of the forty-two members of the Committee received more than one hundred thousand dollars from PACs in 1982, and seventeen more received between fifty thousand and one hundred thousand dollars. Of the forty-two members, ten were just appointed in January, 1983. Business PACs gave nearly twice as much as labor PACs, according to Common Cause. The largest PAC contributors were, not surprisingly, those concerned with the Clean Air Act, telecommunications policy, energy policy, and health issues. (And it is to be remembered that a great deal of special-interest money is given through individual, rather than PAC, contributions; so the PAC listings provide only a partial picture.) PAC contributions to members of the Energy and Commerce Committee as of November, 1982, included, by interest group: $21,000 from commodities exchanges; $3,500 from cotton; $5,500 from grain; $66,235 from the milk industry; $6,835 from poultry and livestock; $6,150 from sugar and sweeteners; $17,450 from other agricultural interests; $104,850 from the auto industry; $65,875 from the chemical industry; $208,322 from communications; $44,800 from computers and electronics; $104,274 from drug companies and medical suppliers; $468,820 from energy; $223,300 from finance; $129,117 from food; $46,025 from forest and paper products; $18,154 from general business interests; $55,897 from the aerospace industry; $113,825 from the insurance industry; $43,050 from metals and mining; $47,150 from machinery and tools; $90,250 from manufacturing; $215,780 from real estate and construction; $57,200 from retail businesses; $33,650 from service industries (hotel, motel, recreation); $46,650 from steel; $14,800 from textiles; $38,525 from tobacco; $131,117 from transportation; $49,500 from dentists; $118,150 from doctors; $71,560 from hospitals; $63,311 from nurses; $15,575 from ideological conservative groups; $3,770 from congressional leaders; $10,405 from environmental groups; $20,025 from gun groups; $13,250 from ideological liberal groups; $8,375 from nonconnected organizations; $17,098 from Presidential hopefuls; $18,137 from miscellaneous political sources; $665,757 from labor; $7,600 from accountants; $59,800 from lawyers; $6,750 from other professionals; $17,900 from engineers; and $41,100 from other miscellaneous sources.

Tim Wirth, forty-three, came to Congress in 1975 as part of the "Watergate class" of reform-minded Democrats. He is a public-spirited person and a smart, substantive politician. He fought a battle to change the 1982 anti-trust agreement between A.T.&T. and the Justice Department. A.T.&T. fought back with a major lobbying effort, and held off congressional action, but later a federal judge changed some of the terms of the agreement in line with some of Wirth's objections. Therefore, the way Wirth became caught up in the logic of the money system is telling.

Wirth, who represents a formerly Republican district that includes Boulder, Colorado, and other areas near Denver, had close elections in his first three races, and in 1980 he won by fifty-six percent. In 1981, he became chairman of the Commerce Committee's Subcommittee on Telecommunications, Consumer Protection, and Finance. The subcommittee deals not only with telecommunications issues but also with federal securities laws, the Securities and Exchange Commission, and automobile safety. One of the biggest matters before Wirth's subcommittee is the revision of the Communications Act of 1934. Since the Act was written, there were revolutionary changes in the telecommunications field, involving big stakes for large interests. Among these were the breakup of A.T.&T., the growth of the cable- and satellite-broadcasting industries, the development of a revolutionary wireless telephone system (cellular radio), and the whole range of computer-information services. Challenge and opportunity made Wirth one of the House's more aggressive money raisers. He once told a group of his colleagues that presiding over a subcommittee offered especially valuable opportunities for fund-raising. A study of the F.E.C. printout of Wirth's campaign contributions offers a virtual *tour d'horizon* of the telecommunications industry, with large sums provided by parties that had an interest in the telecommunications bill. Wirth also received contributions from a number of companies in the securities business. And it is to be remembered that interested parties give as individuals as well as through PACs. In 1982, *Broadcasting* magazine reported that John Saeman, who is the chief executive officer of Daniels & Associates, a cable-television company, and who also serves as the chairman of the National Cable Television Association, held a fund-raiser for Wirth at his Denver home and raised about twenty-five thousand dollars for him. The magazine also reported that in early October a fund-raiser for Wirth was held at "21" by Gustave Hauser, the then-chairman and chief executive officer of Warner Amex Cable Communications. In 1982, Wirth received about five hundred and fifty thousand dollars from individuals, and two hundred and twenty thousand from PACs. He was the top recipient of PAC money on the Committee.

I asked Wirth how he felt about taking so much in campaign contributions from groups over which he has jurisdiction.

He replied, "I'm in the game, and I play by the rules, so it doesn't bother me. The telecommunications types have all kinds of different interests, and they're a diverse group." Wirth also pointed out that he expected to spend about six hundred thousand dollars on his 1982 campaign, because campaigning in Denver requires heavy use of television advertising, and because his opponent had been encouraged to enter the race by the House Republican campaign committee and was receiving the support of such groups as the A.M.A., Standard Oil of Ohio, and the Realtors. (Hedging bets being a common practice, the Realtors also gave to Wirth; but they gave him four hundred dollars and his opponent ten thousand.) In fact, it was estimated all along that Wirth's opponent would be able to raise only about half as much for the campaign as Wirth could, and the general impression was that Wirth was in no real danger. BIPAC did not support Wirth's opponent. For the 1982 election, Wirth spent seven hundred and forty-six thousand dollars, while his opponent spent a hundred and sixteen thousand. Wirth won by sixty-three percent.

Wirth's point that the telecommunications industry has diverse and competing interests has some validity. A similar argument is made by other members of Congress who accept contributions from a variety of parties at interest. The flaw in the argument is that it can assume a universe composed of the parties at interest, and that when the parties at interest carve up the universe everyone is served. Wirth is, as he says, "playing by the rules." One alternative is to take a more relaxed attitude toward raising money—and take a bigger chance on losing. Another alternative is to change the rules.

Philip Sharp, a Democratic representative from Muncie, Indiana, was also elected with the "Watergate class," and he, too, heads a Commerce Committee subcommittee—on Fossil and Synthetic Fuels. In addition, he serves on the Energy and Environment Subcommittee of the House Interior and Insular Affairs Committee. Sharp, who is known in the House as a hardworking member, is inclined to try to fashion legislative compromises. His district had never been safely Democratic, and the Indiana legislature's redistricting made it even more Republican in 1982. Moreover, in 1982 he faced a challenger who had been sponsored by the House Republican campaign committee in what it termed an "opportunity race." BIPAC, too, endorsed Sharp's opponent. So Sharp decided that he had to break with his past practice of declining to take contributions from political-action committees in the energy field. Sharp, who is forty years old, is a soft-spoken, sandy-haired, earnest, but not humorless man. He attended Oxford University and is a former professor.

Sharp talked with me one afternoon before the 1982 election about the difficulty of his decision. He said, "I've always taken PAC money, but never from interests affected by the Energy Subcommittee. Frankly, there was always a problem of drawing the line. In this campaign, we were going to be drowned by money and by reapportionment, so I decided I had to unleash our side. I'm not really worried about my own personal integrity in making an independent judgment, but I am concerned about the question of the perception of me and of the institution. You know, I look at some of the guys on the Banking Committee and the Commerce Committee who take the money and give you the big wink. I wish I could avoid that, and I would have if reapportionment hadn't occurred and if I hadn't been facing the threat of the extraordinary amount of money the Republican committee and the right-wing groups have to spend."

So Sharp set to work raising money. He made phone calls and he held fund-raisers, drawing up his invitation list, as other members of Congress do, from the PAC lists that circulate. (The production and sale of "PAC directories" has become a new industry in Washington. One such book, listing party and non-party contributors and corporate PACs by classification, and PAC support of candidates and interest-group ratings of candidates, weighs nine pounds and costs a hundred and eighty-five dollars.) Sharp sent a mailing to PACs that might contribute to him. He rounded up people who would make calls to PACs on his behalf. Invitations to Sharp's fund-raiser listed the names of House Democratic leaders and members of the Indiana delegation as co-sponsors of the event. He told me, "The problem is that almost every Democrat sends out the same thing. The system is getting pretty worn." As a result of his efforts, Sharp raised money from pipeline companies, utility companies, and producers of oil, natural gas, and coal. Some of the money came in small amounts from organizations that were actually opposing him. "That's the token contribution," he said. "By virtue of being a member of the Commerce Committee, you tend to get that kind of contribution. I think it's clear that because you're chairman of a subcommittee and number six in rank on the Commerce Committee people on both sides of the issue will contribute."

However, some of Sharp's contributions from companies in the energy field were in the thousand-dollar range, and he also received funds from the communications, pharmaceutical, transportation, and financial industries, among others. In all, Sharp received thirty-nine thousand dollars from energy PACs; his opponent, about twenty-five thousand. Sharp also received money from consumer and environmentalist groups, but, he says, "that side doesn't have that many committees or the sort of range that the other side has." Labor also gave Sharp substantial support. Sharp ended up as the recipient of the second-largest amount of PAC money (after Wirth) on the Commerce Committee. In his 1980 campaign, Sharp spent about a hundred and sixty-five thousand dollars. In 1982, he spent three hundred and seventy thousand dollars. His opponent spent two hundred and eighty thousand. (These figures do not count the help given by the national committees.) Sharp was reelected by a relatively comfortable fifty-six percent.

The attractiveness to members of Congress of sitting on certain committees, and to interest groups of having friendly members on those committees, caused quite a scramble when the Ninety-eighth Congress convened in January of 1983. Seats on the Energy and Commerce Committee were the most sought-after. Prospective members were talked of in terms of the interests they appeared to represent: this one represented those who want a strong Clean Air Act; this one the coal industry; this one the oil industry. One newly elected member of Congress was said to be so disturbed by the commitments sought by various interest groups in exchange for their support for his gaining a seat on the committee that he withdrew from the effort. Not everyone was so delicate. One new member approached an official of a major telecommunications company and pledged his everlasting support of the company's interests if the official would help him get on the Committee. The official who had seen a lot, was shocked, and declined to help. Seats on the Ways and Means Committee are also considered valuable, of course. When Barbara Kennelly, a newly elected Democrat from Hartford, Connecticut, won a seat on Ways and Means, one of her colleagues was quoted as saying, "The insurance industry must have a representative on that committee." Representative Carroll Campbell, Republican of South Carolina, made a bid to sit on Ways and Means by stressing that, like Ken Holland, also of South Carolina, who was retiring, he was a strong supporter of the textile industry. Campbell was appointed to the Committee.

11

Why is all this money floating about? What do the investors expect? At a minimum, they expect access, but access is simply the required entry ticket for getting something done. John Culver, the former Democratic senator from Iowa, says, "I think there's no question that money gives you real access. The members have to get their money someplace, and they are grateful for the contributions. All other things being equal, they hope that if you've got a problem they can support your position, and they realize that if they can't they're not going to get any money from you in the future." The young lawyer-lobbyist says, "We are in such a retail business that for a hundred and fifty dollars you can get access. There are some senior members of Congress whose fund-raisers I've gone to, giving a hundred and fifty dollars, and when I call I can get through. I think that if I hadn't given the money it would have been harder. I really believe that anyone who gives a hundred and fifty, two hundred and fifty dollars is treated like a prince. I can imagine how someone who gives a thousand dollars or directs a five-thousand-dollar PAC contribution to someone is treated."

Charles Ferris, who worked as a key Senate Democratic aide for years, then headed the Federal Communications Commission, and is now in private law practice in Washington, says, "A member of Congress's time is very limited. Who do they see? They'll certainly see the ones who gave the money. It's hard to say no to someone who gave you five grand." An aide to the House leadership says, "The first measure of influence around here is access." The aide continued, "Obviously, the most important factor in establishing the legislative outcome is the information that the members are acting upon. Clearly, this has to be viewed in the context of members overburdened with demands on their time. So a little bit of information will carry a member a long way." No less an authority than Justin Dart, one of Ronald Reagan's longtime financial backers and the chairman of Dart Industries, which maintained one of the largest corporate PACs in 1978 and 1980, has said that dialogue with politicians "is a fine thing, but with a little money they hear you better." Senator Inouye says, "The fact remains that when someone gives you a thousand or two thousand dollars he expects that door to be open to him—and he gets a little preferential treatment." He added, "The senator may not be the door-opener himself. But the staff knows who contributed. You have ten people vying for one hour. A staff member will say, 'I think you ought to see Mr. So-and-So and Mr. So-and-So. We'll send letters to the others.' Often, that decision depends on the level of support." Dan Rostenkowski, the chairman of the committee that has jurisdiction over the U.S. tax code, said to me, "A guy gives you a thousand dollars, and his trade is bringing people in the door, and he wants you to talk to them. I do that all the time. You don't want to take a shingle off a guy's roof."

A commonly held view is that the money goes straight toward a legislative outcome—put the money in the slot and out comes a bill. And sometimes that is the case. One of the most spectacular examples—the success of the used-car dealers in 1982 in getting the House and the Senate to vote to overturn a regulation of the Federal Trade Commission that they list the known major defects of an automobile—was almost a caricature of what happens. The automobile dealers spent six hundred and seventy-five thousand dollars in the 1980 campaign—up from just fourteen thousand dollars six years earlier. Of the two hundred and eighty-six House members who voted to kill the F.T.C. regulation, two hundred and forty-two had received money from the auto dealers. "Of course it was money," one House member said to me afterward. "Why else would they vote for used-car dealers?" But the effect of money works on several levels and in many ways, some of them subtle.

The plain truth is that most issues before Congress do not involve great moral principles, and the lobbyists understand that a little persuasion will often do the trick. If an issue doesn't involve a high moral principle, and if it doesn't directly affect an important constituency group, the member is open to persuasion. He who has access is most likely to persuade. Tom Downey, the young representative from New York, says, "It is far too crass to actually buy votes—to say 'Here's ten thousand dollars for your campaign if you vote a certain way.' There are exceptions to this—such as the used-car dealers, who bought their way to happiness. But the more important thing is that if your opponent takes PAC money you have to, and that's bad, because the people who give to you are buying access and influence. Most issues here are not issues of conscience or morality—they are questionable calls. The people with money always have access and always have influence and are capable of tipping the scale. The whole process has become very much distorted by money." The aide to the House leadership says, "The truth is that if you take the most honest member, whoever it might be—someone who's self-conscious about not being overly influenced by campaign contributors—the moment he crosses the threshold of accepting PAC money, or money from large contributors, the whole system is corroded. At that point, the big contributor inevitably has an advantage in terms of access."

Theoretically, a congressman's staff is supposed to protect him from the pressures, and help keep him informed about the merits of an issue, but the staff has become as caught up in the money-raising frenzy as its boss. Says one House aide, "The idealized conception is that the staff acts as a filter and sees to it that the best information is available to the congressman or the senator on most important decisions. But in fact the boss sets the tenor of the office, and if the boss shows by his activities that his concern is with raising money and trying to accommodate those who have raised money in the past, then any normal staff member will try to accommodate that. His boss's priorities become his own. Most staff people are competing for attention and for what is perceived to be the power in a field where there is very little power to go around, so the trappings become very important, and the major trapping is the favor of the boss. The staff wins that by reflecting the boss's interests." And if the boss loses, the staff is out of a job.

Another House aide says, "Context is very important. The common picture is of the members of Congress as marionettes whose strings are pulled by the lobbies, but that's not accurate. Because there are all these pressures on them for reelection, if members take risks on some issues it is common for them to protect themselves on others. The problem is that some very well-meaning, sincere members of Congress enter into these unholy alliances in order to make it possible to get reelected, or to express themselves freely on some matters, and then they find the bonds of the alliance hard to sever." The alliance is not necessarily struck by the money already received, but it's cemented by the need to go back for more. One campaign consultant says, "It's the last-minute money that's the most expensive. The people with the money are just sitting there waiting for you—with big smiles on their faces."

The overturning of the used-car regulation was one of a set of moves that Congress made to try to interfere with regulatory-agency rulings. The legality of the whole procedure is now in question, but if it should continue, this practice, combined with the availability of special-interest money, offers possibilities that are awesome. The legislation killing the used-car rule was unanimously overturned by a Court of Appeals in October, 1982, on the ground that "legislative veto" of actions by regulatory agencies violates the constitutional principle of separation of powers.

Congress has become increasingly interested in the idea of the legislative veto, and moves to overturn agency regulations certainly do attract a lot of money. A move to prevent the F.T.C.

from exercising jurisdiction over price-fixing practices by doctors and dentists attracted two hundred and nineteen House sponsors. Even James Miller, who was appointed chairman of the F.T.C. by the Reagan Administration, which is philosophically against regulation, opposed the move. According to a study made by Public Citizen, a Ralph Nader group, the American Medical Association and the American Dental Association contributed almost $1.3 million in the 1979–80 campaign period; as of mid-October, 1982, the last reporting date for campaign contributions before the issue was voted on, the A.M.A. had contributed $1.5 million, and the American Dental Association more than five hundred thousand. Co-sponsors of the legislation to exempt the medical professions received on the average more than twice as much as those who had not signed on. On December 1, 1982, the House approved the exemption by a vote of 245–155, after rejecting a compromise by a vote of 208–195. The two hundred and eight representatives who voted against the compromise received twice as much money from the two groups as those who supported it. But the bad notices that House action received, plus the determination of Senator Warren Rudman, Republican of New Hampshire, to prevent what he termed "a frontal lobotomy on the free-enterprise system," caused the Senate in mid-December to defeat the exemption of the medical profession.

Elliott Levitas, a Democratic representative from Georgia, has for some years sponsored legislation that would permit Congress to overturn any agency regulation. Even before the Court of Appeals acted, a number of observers believed that this would be terrible public policy. The question of its constitutionality aside, it would drown Congress in dealing with hundreds of regulations, about whose merits it would be largely ignorant. However, business and trade-association groups are enthusiastic about the idea, and are grateful to Levitas. Bernadette Budde, the political-education director of BIPAC, said to me, "To be against Elliott Levitas as a Republican challenger means that if you win you're going to win without the support of the business PACS."

The medical lobbies were instrumental in defeating a major Carter Administration proposal to lower medical costs in this country by imposing a system of hospital-cost containment. The bill was finally defeated in 1979, when the House adopted a substitute sponsored by Gephardt, which called for a study of the problem. Large amounts of money went from the A.M.A. to those members who opposed the cost-containment legislation. (The A.M.A. has been among Gephardt's more generous supporters.) Also involved in the effort to kill the legislation, which would have reduced inflation and Medicare and Medicaid costs, was a kind of health-care consortium consisting of hospital associations and suppliers of health-care products. Those who voted against the hospital-cost-containment proposal received far more in funds from the A.M.A. than those who voted for it—almost four times as much, according to a study by Common Cause. The A.M.A. has also found another way to help its friends—by hiring pollsters for them. As of September, 1982, the A.M.A.'s political-action committee, AMPAC, had spent three hundred and eighty-one thousand dollars to hire pollsters in thirty-six congressional districts.

There are numerous ways besides casting a vote on the House or Senate floor for a member of Congress to show gratitude for a contribution. One, of course, is to cast a vote a certain way in a committee or a subcommittee. Another is to try to block action in a committee or a subcommittee. Another is to cast a vote a certain way on a certain amendment in a subcommittee—or even to refrain from casting a vote—so as to shape a piece of legislation in a certain direction, and then cover one's tracks by voting for approval of the legislation. Still others are to delay a bill until time runs out or to load it up with amendments until it collapses of its own weight. It is not uncommon for a member to say to a colleague, or for a lobbyist to say to a member, "Look, I know you can't be with me on the final bill, but would you do me a favor on this one amendment?" A member may go along out of sheer comradeship, but if he feels an obligation he will try to oblige. The fact that committee meetings (with the exception of those involving national security) are now held in the open—a reform that was adopted in the mid-seventies—has strengthened the lobbyists' hand and reduced the legislators' ability to legislate. The idea was to make the members more accountable for the actions they took in committee, and it was a good one, but it carried a price. The lobbyists used to have to stand around in the corridors and wait to hear about what had happened inside. A member could come out and tell the lobbyist he had done as well as he could for him but couldn't get everything the lobbyist wanted. Members could quietly make trade-offs with each other inside the committee room, where there was at least more of a chance that a member would exercise independent judgment. Now the lobbyists sit right in the committee room, keeping score. Sometimes they even signal to a member how to vote on a certain amendment. During the House-Senate conference between members of the Ways and Means and Finance Committees on the 1982 tax-increase bill, the large Ways and Means Committee room had an overflow crowd.

12

The scramble for money can have two effects: it can propel legislation along that in earlier years would not have seen the light of day, and it can paralyze legislation. A bill that one interest group feels strongly about and has made a substantial investment in, and that encounters no strong countervailing force, has a good chance of being enacted. The overturning of the used-car rule is but one example. On the other hand, if there are strong factions in contention the result can be legislative deadlock. Sometimes this occurs because members strongly committed to one contender or the other cannot reach a compromise. Sometimes it occurs because members courted by both sides would rather not make a decision. A man who has served as a staff member on Capitol Hill for many years said to me as we sat in his office one afternoon in the fall of 1982, "This is the worst Congress I have ever seen." He said that he had been in a depression over what he had seen. He said, "We have more special-interest legislation; we have more good people sponsoring lousy legislation. The only reason can be their need for and the availability of funds. You have people sponsoring legislation that they really ought not to be sponsoring, in terms of their political anchors. You see them sponsoring changes in antitrust legislation in order to get people to give them money. And they are behaving differently. They are pushier about this bad legislation. Members used to come into committee meetings with open minds, seeking information. The new members come in already bought, and they are advocates rather than judges."

The special-interest bill that suddenly has some two hundred and eighteen sponsors—most of whom don't have a clue to what is in it—is an increasingly common phenomenon. The staff member said, "Members are less and less willing to be specialists. Now they all want to be generalists—and they know less. And the reason this is happening is that they're being importuned so much by the lobbyists and the PACS. They can no longer say, 'I'm not on that committee. I'll wait to see what that committee says. That's not my bag.' Members used to come to Congress and get expertise in a certain area, and other members would trust their judgment. They didn't go putting their names on a lot of bills they didn't know anything about and try to ram the bills through, and they didn't try to rewrite bills on the floor. All that's out the window now." Another House aide says, "The most disturbing situation is where the interest group is success-ful in forcing something through that is never carefully exam-ined and is not understood. In a sense, the interests threaten to displace the committee system." In a sense, the interest groups *have* displaced the congressional committee system: they write the bills and they sign up so many co-sponsors that the commit-tee system is irrelevant.

On September 15, 1982, the House of Representatives passed a bill that largely exempted the shipping industry from anti-trust laws. The bill came roaring out of the Merchant Marine and Fisheries Committee and was referred to the Judiciary Committee, which sent it to the House floor, where it was taken up under a procedure that provides for limited debate. Toward the end of the "debate," Peter Rodino, the chairman of the House Judiciary Committee, said that it had been called to his attention "a few minutes ago" that the bill removed the Justice Department's authority to litigate maritime matters, but that "we are not in a position to correct this problem now." The bill passed the House by a vote of 350–33. Senator Metzenbaum blocked its passage in the Senate.

The Malt Beverage Interbrand Competition Act, a bill that would exempt brewers from anti-trust laws so that distributors could have monopolies on certain brands in certain parts of the country—any bill whose title contains the word "competition" is usually designed to bring about the opposite—had two hundred and eighty-two sponsors in the House and sixty-six sponsors in the Senate. The backing of the brewing industry, and of the National Beer Wholesalers' Association, which formed a political-action committee called SIXPAC, gave the bill a certain attractiveness to members of Congress, despite the fact that it was likely to raise the price of beer. A bill to change the bankruptcy code had two hundred and seventy-nine sponsors in the House. This bill, called the Bankruptcy Improvements Act, would establish a vastly harsher system of treating individuals who have declared bankruptcy. The approach has been rejected by Congress many times, and was rejected by a Presidential commission in 1972, but in the Ninety-seventh Congress it came within range of passing. Nearly a million dollars was contributed by interested groups. Among the powerful groups behind it are banks, credit unions, finance companies, savings-and-loan institutions, and some large retail chains, including Sears, Roebuck. A bill to require that automobiles sold in the United States contain a specified percentage of American parts, or a specified percentage be assembled by American labor (the "domestic content" bill), was passed by the House at the behest of the U.A.W., despite deep misgivings on the part of many people who voted for it. Though they feared that such a policy would set off a trade war and end up costing the nation jobs, they overcame their misgivings. According to Common Cause, the two hundred and fifteen members who voted for the bill had received $1.3 million from the U.A.W. between 1979 and 1982.

On the other hand, political-action-committee money was helpful in getting Congress to block a proposal by the Reagan Administration to impose a user fee—of up to twelve cents—on commodity-trade transactions. The fee would pay most of the costs of the federal Commodity Futures Trading Commission; a similar fee on securities transactions helps pay the costs of the Securities and Exchange Commission. The Commodity Commission, which is now largely financed from general revenue, was scheduled to cost twenty-four million dollars in the fiscal year 1983. By June of 1982, the interested parties (except for the taxpayers)—the Chicago Board of Trade, the Chicago Mercantile Exchange, and the Commodity Exchange of New York—had distributed more than three hundred and forty thousand dollars to Senate and House candidates, the *Wall Street Journal* reported, and had five hundred and thirty thousand more to distribute before the November elections. According to the *Journal*, donations were given to all but three members of the House Agriculture Committee, which rejected the fee proposal, and to two-thirds of the Senate Agriculture Committee, which also rejected it. When Senator William Roth, Republican of Delaware, offered it on the Senate floor, it was defeated by a vote of sixty-six to twenty-seven.

Among the more favored recipients were Senators Richard Lugar, Republican of Indiana (fifteen thousand dollars), and Donald Riegle, Democrat of Michigan (eight thousand dollars), both of whom were up for reelection in 1982. (Lugar chaired the subcommittee that rejected the fee proposal.) On the House side, Representative Marty Russo, Democrat of Illinois, who had tried (unsuccessfully) to help commodities traders retain favored tax treatment (the "butterfly straddle"—a complicated tax maneuver used to get artificial tax losses), received nine thousand two hundred and fifty dollars. Thomas Foley, of Washington, the second-ranking Democrat on the House Agriculture Committee, who frequently has tight reelection races, received six thousand eight hundred dollars. Foley is also the House Majority Whip. Jim Wright, the House Majority Leader, received six thousand dollars. Tony Coelho received four thousand dollars. Moreover, Robert Dole, the second-ranking Republican on the Senate Agriculture Committee as well as chairman of the Finance Committee, received ten thousand dollars for his political-action committee, Campaign America.

Some pieces of legislation have strong contending forces on both sides, and every lawyer-lobbyist in Washington seems to have been signed up by one side or the other. One lawyer-lobbyist says, "That's why the legislators are paralyzed on some of the issues. They just don't want to make a decision if they can avoid it." A piece of legislation that led to what became known as the Lobbyists' Superbowl involved the liability of companies found to have violated the anti-trust laws—an issue involving hundreds of millions of dollars. According to the lawyer-lobbyist, "That bill probably isn't going anywhere, because the lobbyists have paralyzed the members." The Ninety-seventh Congress adjourned at the end of 1982 without taking action on it. Another example is the argument over whether royalties should be paid for the home taping of televised movies and programs and of records. The battle pits the movie, television, and record industries against the Sony Corporation and other manufacturers of videotaping machines and the distributors of videotapes. The list of the lobbyists involved reads like a *Who's Who* of Washington lobbyists, and includes several former members of the House and Senate, two former chairmen of the Federal Communications Commission, and, inevitably, Robert Strauss, Thomas Boggs, and J. D. Williams. This one finds Eizenstat, his former White House deputy, David Rubenstein, and Thomas Boggs and Charles Ferris on the side of the manufacturers, and Strauss, Williams, Jack Valenti, and Dean Burch (like Ferris, a former F.C.C. chairman) on the side of the entertainment industry. Also on this side are Robert Gray, who was formerly of Hill & Knowlton, the public-relations firm, and was co-chairman of Reagan's Inauguration; and Anne Wexler, who handled liaison with oustide groups for the Carter Administration and subsequently began her own lobbying firm. Obviously, most of these people could reach out for reinforcement to major fund raisers. The movie industry is especially interested in the issue, of course, and it seems that no one is more interested than Lew Wasserman, the head of MCA. After one senator seeking reelection made the trek to California in search of funds, and Lew Wasserman was helpful, the senator suddenly expressed interest in the charging of royalties for taping films. "The turnaround time was very short," says one of his fellow senators. "He was barely off the plane." One lobbyist said to me last fall, "If both Strauss and Boggs have held fund-raisers for a senator who is up for reelection, you get the classic result—the senator is undecided." The battle was stalled while the issue went before the Supreme Court, which heard arguments on the case early in 1983. But the pause was only temporary: everyone assumed that it would resume once the Court ruled. The lobbyist added, "For not all that much money, members get frozen. In the end, if it comes to a vote they'll cast a vote, but they would certainly prefer not to do so before the election." He added, "When issues are not issues of conscience—and most of them are not—and their district or state doesn't have a clear interest, if you raise enough money you can keep them from doing anything."

Mike Synar, a thirty-two-year-old Democratic representative from Oklahoma, a moderate, and a member of the House Energy and Commerce Committee, said to me one afternoon in late September, 1982, "The Commerce Committee hasn't passed a major bill in two years. You have some very fine examples of paralysis there." He offered as examples what happened with the Clean Air Act and the telecommunications bill. In the case of the Clean Air Act, which was before the committee for revision in 1982, he said, "The stalemate has been caused fifty percent by industry and fifty percent by environmentalists. Congressmen on the committee said, 'Hey, do we really have to act on this this year?' It's a total mess, and very frustrating." The bill was not acted on in 1982. The stalling on the telecommunications bill was largely the work of A.T.&T., which managed to get it filibustered while conducting a lobbying campaign against it until the Committee gave up.

Synar, who himself refuses to take money from PACs, added, "We have three problems. Most of us are physically and intellectually exhausted from doing the work here and running home most weekends to campaign, so you have a tired Congress that can't concentrate. Second, starting early this year members

didn't want to deal with anything with tough economic interests involved, because they had to raise PAC money and didn't
want to make any PACS mad. So Congress was red meat before
the special interests. They could go to members and say, 'You
don't have to deal with that this year.' Third, you get PACS fighting PACS, so it is just easier to do nothing." He concluded, "Tell
me something major we've done in the last two years, other
than vote on budgets and taxes. It's bad, it's really bad."

One device increasingly used for steering money toward—or,
more important, against—a candidate is the report card. The
report card has become a major source of anxiety among the
politicians, and is yet another blow to the political process. An
interest group keeps score on certain roll-call votes—even sees
to it that issues arise in a form that it can keep score on—and
then sends out mailings showing who voted "wrong," and raising money against them. Moreover, the meaning of the vote is
often distorted. David Obey says, "You get two kinds of money
in politics. Sometimes people feel that if they can buy you early
they'll be in good shape after you get here. The other is that if
they agree with you they'll try to to keep you here, and if they
don't they'll try to bounce you out. Today, we have the situation
where there are threats based on individual votes. Ten thousand
dollars may come in against you from one group because of a
single vote." He also says, "Voters have less and less ability to
understand what the overall record is, and what the individual
legislator is doing to and for them, because you have all these
messages beamed at them on individual issues. So the center
can't hold. We all know that certain roll calls are staged—and
this process adds to the fragmentation. These groups devour
you. Representatives used to think that if they did their job and
represented their districts pretty well they'd be all right. Now
they know that overnight fifty to a hundred thousand dollars
can move into their districts against them."

Among the groups that get out report cards is the National
Federation of Independent Business, one of the organizations

that work closely with the Republican Party leadership. The N.F.I.B. is run by James McKevitt, a former Republican representative from Colorado. The N.F.I.B. scorecard rated House members on four roll-call votes in 1981, all of them related to support of Reagan's economic program. Synar says, "The N.F.I.B. gave me a zero rating—for four votes, out of *all* the votes I cast last year." One hundred Democrats complained to the N.F.I.B. that these votes hardly constituted a test of support for small business, and that the Democratic tax and budget proposals would have been more beneficial to it. Synar says, "All those Main Street people know is that I rate a zero. The Independent Petroleum Association of America also gave me a zero—on the basis of two votes. I helped get them a provision in the Democratic tax-cut bill, but because I didn't vote for the President's bill, which had the identical provision in it, and because of a vote on a procedural matter on the tax bill, I got a zero." This was the oil provision that was part of the bidding war. Synar concluded, "So I'm competing against the special interests, not the Republican Party."

The tradition of interest groups' rating members' voting records is an old one, but the ratings by such groups as Americans for Democratic Action, COPE, the National Association of Businessmen, and Americans for Constitutional Action are based on a broad sample of issues. What is new is scorecards based on a very few votes, sometimes deliberately staged and then misinterpreted. Moreover, it is not just conservative groups that use scorecards on specific subjects as instruments of attack. One environmental group, Environmental Action, used to proclaim the congressmen who had done worst by its standards the "Dirty Dozen." The National Organization for Women spent a half-million dollars in the 1982 congressional elections, based not on a scorecard but on a set of specific issues, including economic issues as well as the abortion issue and the Equal Rights Amendment. (NOW spent another one million dollars on state legislature races.) A new group called PeacePAC spent money against congressmen (the "Doomsday Dozen") on the basis of their votes on the use of chemical weapons, the MX, and the nuclear freeze.

The National Association of Realtors uses the report card in a novel, and highly controversial, way. It rates members not simply on how they vote but on presumed implications—in terms of jobs lost, the inflation rate, and so on—of their votes. The roll calls that are selected favor Republicans, and several have little noticeable relation to housing. The Realtors also subject congressional candidates to a questionnaire, forcing them to commit themselves on issues before they get to Congress. The Realtors' other device for wielding influence is money—enormous amounts of money. The Realtors distributed $1.6 million in 1980 (compared to six thousand seven hundred dollars ten years earlier). In 1982, the Realtors Association contributed $2.3 million, making it the largest spender of the PACs. The Realtors were also planning to spend three and a half million or so in state elections. A number of PACs, like the national party committees, establish state funds, which can use corporate—soft—money. (A number of these also use soft money to pay honorariums to members of Congress who speak before them.) The Realtors' main interest was in supporting the Reagan Administration's moves to cut the budget and bring down interest rates. The association did not, however, let philosophy get in the way of its own interests in the case of the 1982 tax-increase bill. It succeeded, along with the Direct Selling Association, with which it is allied in NAFAPAC, in getting its members exempted from provisions in the bill that would have treated them as employees for the purposes of withholdings and Social Security. While the thrust of the 1982 tax-increase bill was to speed up and tighten up the collection of taxes, realtors and direct sellers were exempted from any such provisions. Having won their exemption, the Realtors supported the 1982 tax bill, and helped the White House get it passed. Richard Thaxton, the Realtors' vice-president for political affairs, told me that his organization planned to be involved in three hundred and fifty congressional races in 1982—which covers a lot of ground.

But the participation would be of different orders of enthusiasm. The obligatory contribution—of five thousand dollars—was made to the worry-free Rostenkowski. But most of the money goes to conservatives. A contribution of five thousand dollars was made to Representative Kent Hance, Democrat of Texas, even though he had no real election problem; Hance had been a key figure in putting together the conservative coalition that got the President's budget through the House. Then, there are other reasons for the Realtors' contributing. Thaxton says, "We go to an awful lot of receptions. We look at that as access money: 'We know you're there and casting votes, and we'd like to be able to talk to you.' Then, there are the races where we'll give a thousand dollars or more. Thirty percent of our money will go to Democrats and seventy percent to Republicans. But in terms of the numbers we give to, it's fifty-fifty, because the Democrats control the House and we go to a lot of two-hundred-and-fifty-dollar receptions. I can legitimately say to my Democratic friends that fifty percent of our giving is to Democrats, and I can legitimately say to my Republican friends that seventy percent of our money goes to Republicans. It's two different questions."

13

It is often said that what is driving the chase for money on the part of candidates for Congress is the ever-increasing cost of campaigning, but that gets it backward. What is driving the chase for money is its own momentum. It is the domestic equivalent of the arms race. A candidate feels compelled to spend so much money because his opponent is spending so much, or might spend so much, or groups intent on his defeat might spend so much. Of course, the costs of the components of campaigns—polling, consultants, direct mail, and, most of all, television time—have risen; but the sum total of what is spent on campaigns has risen because the political system as it now functions has allowed, even encouraged, it to. A candidate for office doesn't set out to spend a half million or a million dollars for the sheer joy of it; he does it because he fears the consequences of not doing it. And unless he is independently wealthy he has to raise that money—or be more vulnerable to defeat. It is not accidental that the number of independently wealthy people entering politics is rising. And the quest for money has distended and distorted the political system to the point where it bears little resemblance to what it was supposed to be.

A candidate entering politics now must systematically make the rounds of the interest groups and win their approval, and their money, by declaring himself, usually in very specific terms, in favor of the legislative goals they seek. He is therefore imprisoned before he ever reaches Congress. Once there, he must worry about maintaining the groups' support or about finding other groups to support him or about casting some vote that might cause monetary retaliation. He must measure every action in terms of what the financial consequences to himself might be. The difference between that and corruption is unclear.

When Jonathan Bingham, a Democratic representative from New York, retired from Congress in December, 1982, after eighteen years in service, he held a farewell press conference at which he drew a distinction between what he saw as the old and the new corruption. Bingham had been elected to Congress after defeating Charles Buckley, a Bronx Democratic leader and congressman. "I never heard anyone say that Charles Buckley was available for contributions," Bingham said at his press conference. "His was a different kind of corruption, but in some ways better. On the important votes he voted correctly. Yes, he had his organization and his committee staff in the Bronx who never went to Washington. His was old-style Tammany Hall—what George Washington Plunkitt [a Tammany politician] called 'honest graft.'" Bingham said that the new corruption was "hard to pin down." He said, "I think it's the rare case of 'We'll contribute if you vote so and so.' It's just that they have access. If you have strong pressure coming from a particular group, it's likely to frustrate the process." In the closing days of the Ninety-seventh Congress, Bingham introduced a constitutional amendment that would allow Congress to set limits on campaign expenditures, thus overturning a portion of the Supreme Court's decision in *Buckley* v. *Valeo*. (However, if a law were enacted establishing public financing of congressional campaigns, according to the Buckley decision such a constitutional amendment would not be necessary.) Bingham said that he was introducing the amendment as a catalyst for debate.

Two other members of Congress talked about what they termed the "corruption" upon their retirement at the end of 1982. In an appearance on "Meet the Press," Representative Millicent Fenwick, Republican of New Jersey, spoke of "the danger of perceived or actual corruption," which was, she said, "far more serious, I think, than the public is aware." She added, "When a complete stranger or almost complete stranger will tell you quite frankly, 'Yes, I'm going to vote that way, because I took fifty-eight thousand from such-and-such a group and they want it,' I call that corruption." Henry Reuss, Democrat of Wisconsin, said, "The corruption and the evil is not only in people seeming to sell access or in some cases perhaps even their votes; it lies in the preoccupation of legislators, many of them very fine men and women, who have to spend a large part of their lives pan-handling, going around to all these groups saying, 'I would just love to have a check from you.' That shouldn't be."

An argument is sometimes made that since everyone is in the game—since all the interests are raising and distributing money—it all evens out in the end. But, for one thing, the premise is not true. As Robert Dole says, "there aren't any Poor PACs or Food Stamp PACs or Nutrition PACs or Medicare PACs." Moreover, comparisons between spending by business and by labor are misleading, because often business is fighting busi-ness, and sometimes, as in the case of a weapons system or construction project (the B-1 bomber, the Clinch River Breeder Reactor), business and labor are on the same side. Senator Dale Bumpers, Democrat of Arkansas, says, "You can't have a sensi-ble debate about how much is enough for defense when those PACs are contributing so much. The decisions aren't based on what the likely mission of the Pentagon is going to be." And, even if the premise were true, the logical conclusion of the argument that there is no problem because everyone is in on the game is that the political system should go to the highest bidder.

The point about everyone being in the game also lacks rele-vance because, irrespective of who is winning or losing, the real problem is what the system does to the politicians. We now have a system in which even the best-intentioned politicians get caught up in either actual or apparent conflicts of interest, in which it is difficult to avoid in effect selling votes for campaign contributions. We have a system in which even the best people do these things, not because they want to but because they are trapped. After every election, we get analyses showing that not everyone who spends more money wins. Of course not; there are numerous factors in a campaign, ranging from the state of the economy to what might be termed the "jerk factor"— having to do with the quality of the candidates. But money can make the difference in what would otherwise be a close race.

Politicians on Capitol Hill have a little joke that goes, "I'm a man of principle. Once I'm bought, I stay bought." It is a fact that special-interest money as a percentage of campaign funds has grown. Increasingly, the shape and nature of our politics is being determined by the interests that have the money to con- tribute and the technicians who instruct the candidates in how to raise it and use it. Increasingly, the question of who gets funds is a decision made within Washington, by people who have an eye on some piece of the national agenda. The young lawyer-lobbyist says, "The interests run this city; everyone knows it." A member of Congress says, "The lobbyists set the national agenda." Some of the interest groups talk about how their political decisions are made at the "grass roots," but of course that, for the most part, is nonsense. Their Washington representatives are paid to monitor, and try to influence, the behavior of the politicians in Washington. Politicians are forced to respond less and less to their constituents and more and more to the interests with the money. The money flows into a district or a state at the direction of interests that have little or nothing to do with the area. Campaigns are increasingly cen- tralized in Washington by the technicians and the money men. The more money that is involved in the political process, the more important the technological decisions become, and, in a circular way, the more important money becomes. One lobbyist says that the role of money is what has led to so many "plastic politicians"—politicians groomed for the television age (some- times known as the "blow-dried politicians"), whose beliefs are malleable. The Democratic pollster Patrick Caddell says, "What worries me is what technology—the pollsters and the technicians—has done to the system. We pick the candidates, and we say what works on television. We're the arbitrators. We say what fits the mold, and we reject the mavericks."

It is the role of money that has given us, increasingly, politicians who are exhausted, who can't think clearly, who don't think about broad questions—don't have the time, even if they have the inclination, to do so. Who don't lead. The Burkean ideal—the ideal of the politician leading his constituents, rather than simply reacting to "the convenience of the hour"—is not just diminishing as a factor in our politics; it has almost disappeared. The role of money has delivered us into the special-interest state. As Jim Leach, the Republican congressman from Iowa, says, we have "a breakdown of constitutional democracy, which is supposed to be based upon citizen access and constituency access." Dale Bumpers says, "Money is the number-one political problem our country is facing. I know that money distorts the democratic process." There are things that can be done to help restore the process to its original purpose, and they will be gone into later. First, we have to decide whether we want to try to restore the political process to its original purpose.

14

The idea that Presidential campaigns have been freed from private money and that the candidates proceed on an equal financial footing is a myth. The laws governing the contributions and expenditures for Presidential campaigns started out in workable form, and constituted a profound change, but then they became riddled with loopholes—one of them, according to Robert Keefe, the Democratic consultant, "big enough to drive a President through." Richard Wirthlin, the pollster for Ronald Reagan's 1980 Presidential campaign, says, "My own feeling is that the law hasn't changed the access to resources; it's simply changed the channels that are used to get those resources into the campaign." Wirthlin was talking of both congressional and Presidential campaigns.

One new channel is provided by the so-called independent committees—committees established for the purpose of raising and spending money on a Presidential candidate's behalf, and supposedly independent of the official campaign. These independent committees are different from political-action committees (PACS), which can make direct contributions to a number of candidates, although some PACS—particularly the ideological ones—also conduct large-scale "independent" activities in both Presidential and congressional campaigns. Another new channel takes the form of soft money—money that cannot legally be spent in federal campaigns. Soft money—union dues, corporate-treasury money, and individual contributions beyond the federal limits—played an important, if largely unnoticed, role in the 1980 campaign. In addition to these new ways of raising and spending money for a Presidential campaign, there are also ways in which large amounts of party money can be spent to uneven the balance. The 1974 campaign finance law, which established a system of public financing of Presidential campaigns as well as set limits on what could be contributed to and spent by a congressional candidate, changed fundamentally the system by which Presidential campaigns were financed. Under the 1974 Act, candidates for the Presidential nomination received federal matching funds for part of the money they raised in individual contributions—which are limited to one thousand dollars from an individual and five thousand dollars from a political-action committee—and were subject to limits on what they could spend in each state. By far, most of the money for the nomination is raised from individuals rather than PACs, which are, for the most part, disinclined to get involved in nomination fights. The only substantial amount of PAC money in the Democratic nomination struggle comes from unions; but the unions' greater contribution is in manpower. Still, the issue of PACs had become sufficiently prominent by early 1983 that Senator Gary Hart, Democrat of Colorado, announced that he would decline to take PAC money in his forthcoming campaign for the Democratic nomination, and would press for campaign-finance reform. Walter Mondale, who had already made campaign-finance reform one of his major themes, said that he, too, would turn down PAC money. This move represented less of a sacrifice for Hart than it did for Mondale, who was in a strong position to receive the endorsements of the National Education Association and the A.F.L.-C.I.O. Mondale stood to lose a half-million dollars, according to his aides. But Mondale's action was not without value; it would, it was hoped, reduce the prospect of his being seen—if he received the valuable labor endorsements—as the "tool" of the Democratic interests. (Reubin Askew, a former governor of Florida and a Democratic candidate, also said that he would reject PAC money.) If a candidate for the nomination chose not to accept federal funds—as John Connally did in 1980—he was still subject to the contribution limits, but not the spending limits. Once a candidate was nominated, he received a certain amount from the federal government for his campaign—$29.4 million in 1980—and could receive no private contributions. The 1974 Act limited independent expenditures on behalf of any candidate to a thousand dollars. The scheme was paid for by a voluntary dollar checkoff on tax returns. The system, like the rest of the campaign-finance law, was to be supervised by a Federal Election Commission.

One Presidential campaign—the 1976 campaign—was fought on roughly equal financial terms after the 1974 law went into effect. But this campaign was followed both by some changes in the law and by increasing ingenuity in getting around the law. The result was a striking imbalance in what the two parties spent in 1980—an imbalance in the Republican Party's favor. No one argues that Ronald Reagan defeated Jimmy Carter because of Reagan's advantage in money. But the 1980 campaign offers an object lesson in the ways in which outside money can once again play a big role in the Presidential campaign and, unless the laws are changed, will continue to. In an election that is otherwise close, this could make the difference. The 1980 election and subsequent events also indicate that large contributors and fund raisers are rewarded with ambassadorships and other important positions. In effect, the Presidential-campaign reforms that followed the Nixon scandals have to a large extent been nullified. And if the past is any guide, what was done in 1980 to get around the law will be amplified in the future.

One of the Republicans' major financial advantages in 1980 grew out of the change that had been made in the federal election law the year before, which allowed state and local party organizations to spend unlimited amounts for voter registration and for getting out the vote in Presidential elections. It also allowed the local party organizations to spend unlimited amounts on the paraphernalia of campaigns—bumper stickers, billboards, and the like—and on expenses connected with volunteer activities. The high-minded rationale for the change was that in 1976 so much of the federal money given to the Presidential candidates had gone into television advertising that the role of state and local parties, of "grass roots" activity, had been severely diminished. Though it can be argued that spending the money on television was the decision of the national campaigns, and that most of the money will always go into television, and so be it, the case was made to Congress that it was its solemn duty to encourage "party-building activities."

But beneath the high-minded rationale were some tactical calculations being made by both parties. Just as in 1974, when changes were made in the election law which led to the explosion of political-action committees, the Democrats and their labor-union allies thought that the 1979 change in the Presidential-election law would work in their favor. And, just as in 1974, they were mistaken. The 1979 change was pushed largely by Morley Winograd, who at the time was the chairman of the Democratic Party in Michigan, where the United Auto Workers and the state party had a very close relationship, and who was also president of the association of Democratic state-party chairmen. The theory was that money that could not otherwise be spent in federal elections, such as union dues—soft money—could be channelled into the all-important voter-turnout activities conducted in the states. (Before the law was changed, the Federal Election Commission had held that such activities on behalf of any federal candidate would be tightly controlled; the parties wanted to get these activities out from under any federal supervision.) The Democrats figured that to work with the unions, using union money, to get out the vote, was a natural Democratic thing. What they didn't figure on was that raising big money was not a Democratic thing but a Republican thing, and that the Republicans would be alert to the opportunity that the change in the law provided. Patrick Caddell, the Democratic pollster, says, "Everyone said, 'What a great idea. We're going to help Morley and the U.A.W.' The only state party that was benefitted by this was Michigan. It wasn't until too late that we realized we were going to be outspent."

What was not contemplated by the congressional sponsors of the change was the raising and distributing of large sums of soft money at the national level—that a supposedly state-party activity would be taken over by the national committees and used as a way of infusing money raised nationally into the states. The Republican National Committee had already been looking for an opening through which to make additional expenditures in the publicly financed Presidential campaign. Robert Perkins, who had been finance director of the Republican National Committee in 1977 and 1978, says that the Republican Party was eager to get the provision into the law. "We were very excited about it," Perkins recalls. "We knew we needed a big, coordinated, sophisticated operation." And after the change was made, that is the kind of operation the Republicans mounted. The Republicans argue that the change in the law was necessary in order to offset the indirect help that the Democrats received as a result of union efforts to get their members registered and to the polls. While there is no question that unions had been helpful to Democrats in that respect, virtually every Democrat one can find will say (though never for attribution) that the unions are not always as effective as Republicans—and the unions— would have people think. It has been a truism in politics for some time that labor does not necessarily "deliver the vote." It especially doesn't deliver the vote when its constituents are unenthusiastic about the Democratic candidate, as they were in 1980. (In 1982, labor did turn out, because it had an issue to rally around—unemployment.) Reagan received more than forty percent of the labor vote in 1980. But the Republicans like to invoke the spectre of the unions—in fact, they almost need to do so—in order to keep up the pressure to raise money. Labor, in turn, invokes the spectre of "big business."

Perkins says that in 1980 he suggested the idea for a national drive to raise soft money for the Presidential campaign to

William Timmons, the then Reagan campaign political director, in charge of field operations, and now Washington lobbyist. According to Perkins, Timmons said, "Let's run with it." Systematically, they raised large sums of money from individuals and corporations, and funnelled it into the states where it would have the most impact. Under the public-financing law, of course, there are supposed to be no individual contributions to the candidates once they are nominated. Perkins, who is thirty-five, is now the executive vice-president of Polygon, a company that deals in diamonds. He ran the soft-money operation on a part-time basis, out of an office at the Republican National Committee. The laws vary from state to state on the spending of union and corporate money; many states, including some of the most populous ones—California, New York, Illinois—do permit such spending. In all, twenty-eight states permit corporate contributions and forty-one states permit labor contributions. (In some instances, there are limits on one or both categories.) The limits on individual contributions also vary from state to state (twenty-five states, including Texas, have no such limits). But the state restrictions presented no particular problems for the Republicans. For example, Missouri allowed corporate money, but Texas did not. So money that the Republicans raised from individuals in Missouri would be sent to Texas, and money that was raised from corporations in Texas—of which there was quite a bit—was sent to Missouri or California or any of the other states that permitted corporate funds to be used. And there were in effect no limits on what the parties could funnel into the states for voter-registration and get-out-the-vote drives. Perkins says, "We tried to raise money for the states where voter identification and get-out-the-vote would have the most impact. Pennsylvania, Florida, and Texas were high on the list. As the program got rolling and we got successful, we went down the list."

The directions on where to send the money, Perkins says, came from Timmons and his deputy, Stan Anderson. Perkins says, "We picked out the states that needed the money, identified money from major contributors, and funnelled it into the states. This was outside any federal limits; there were no federal limits on these contributions." Thus, a contributor could give unlimited sums from his own corporation or his own pocket for the state drives, to be distributed as the Reagan campaign and Republican Party officials saw fit. And so there are still no limits on the amount of money an individual can give to help elect a President. Someone who wished to could give a hundred thousand dollars or more to each of several state parties in order to get out the vote for his candidate. The money is not counted as a contribution, and is therefore not reported at the federal level. The state reporting requirements vary in stringency.

In other words, contributions of the size that were given to the Nixon campaign of 1972 and that so shocked the nation—and paved the way for public financing of Presidential campaigns—can still be made. And the contributions by corporations which were illegal then can now be made legally. The only difference is that the methods by which the money is contributed are more circuitous. Robert Keefe, who headed the Democrats' soft-money drive, says, "People used to spend large amounts to elect a President. I'm not sure we've left that." A Washington Democratic lawyer-lobbyist says, "Soft money is where rich people can play again." He adds, "There's nothing to keep me from putting a million dollars into a campaign if I wanted to." A former official of the Federal Election Commission says, "It's a fraud on the American people, who think we have a totally federally funded Presidential campaign." Perkins says that his soft-money drive raised nine million dollars. (Other Republican Party soft money is raised from large contributors who prefer to give corporate, rather than personal, funds.) Paul Dietrich, who is the president of the Fund for a Conservative Majority, an independent political-action committee that worked on Reagan's behalf in 1980, and who also ran the Republican National Committee's state-fund operation in Missouri in 1980, says, "The Republican state operation made a mockery of the law."

What soft money could be used for was fairly loosely defined in 1980 (and the definition has become even looser since then). For example, it could go to cover the expenses of volunteers. The Republicans got a ruling from the F.E.C. that volunteers could be reimbursed by as much as thirty dollars a day for their "expenses." This amounted to more than they would have been paid under the minimum wage—which is what the Democrats were paying people, out of the Party's own "hard money" funds, to run phone banks. (And, unlike the Republican "volunteers," the Democratic workers had to pay taxes on their income.) The work of an advance man who went into a state to set up a rally could be paid for with soft money by charging it off as "coordinating volunteers." So could the work of volunteers who stuffed envelopes for direct-mail campaigns or prepared material for rallies.

Lyn Nofziger, the longtime Reagan political aide who is now a Washington consultant, says, "In a state where it's allowed, you get corporate money and spend it for damn near anything. And if I give fifty thousand dollars in corporate funds in California, that frees the campaign to spend fifty thousand dollars for whatever it wants." To the extent that soft money goes to the parties to pay for their state activities or, as is also permitted, to pay for the costs of their headquarters, this allows other money to be used for other purposes. Timmons says, "It doesn't make much difference what you can use it for, because it frees up your other money."

In 1980, the Republican National Committee raised $2.2 million in soft money to pay for the Eisenhower Center, a four-story brick building on Capitol Hill that houses the national committee and the National Republican Congressional Committee. (In 1982, Mr. and Mrs. Averell Harriman loaned the Democratic Congressional Campaign Committee three hundred and ninety thousand dollars to buy a building on Capitol Hill, to be used as a radio and television studio. The Republicans have had such a facility for ten years.) Soft-money contributions for building funds do not have to be reported to the F.E.C.

The funds raised by Republicans in soft money were used in the states *in addition to* money raised by the state parties—

which was itself substantial. The Texas state party alone, under the enthusiastic leadership of Governor William Clements, raised three million dollars, and it is estimated that another three million dollars was raised by the local parties in Dallas and Houston. In fact, the first trip the Reagan-Bush team made after the nominating Convention was to Houston, to encourage the Republican Party's fund-raising efforts. Reagan returned to Houston for a fund-raiser in mid-September. It was estimated that in some other states, such as New York and California, the Republicans raised at least one million dollars. In other words, the Presidential and Vice-Presidential nominees are still involved in fund-raising in the general election—in a system that is ostensibly paid for with public financing. They encourage people to give to both the national and state parties. The only thing they can't do is ask people to give to their own campaigns—at least directly.

Under another section of the law, the national parties are permitted to spend a certain amount per voter per state (two cents per voter) in a Presidential campaign. The Presidential campaign organization directs how the money is spent. In 1980, under this provision, each party was allowed to spend another $4.6 million on the Presidential race. But it is artificial to make distinctions between what the national parties can spend for Presidential, as opposed to non-Presidential, candidates. Whatever helps the ticket helps the Presidential nominees. John Sears, who managed Reagan's 1976 effort to obtain the Republican nomination and managed the 1980 effort until he was ousted in a power struggle in February, says, "Quite clearly, the Party can do all kinds of things that are of benefit to the Presidential candidate and that are counted as Party functions for the ticket at large—such as polling, fund-raising, running phone banks. People are getting more sophisticated about writing off spending to those activities. So there are all sorts of ways of getting around the limits of what a Presidential candidate can spend."

Therefore, the sum total of what each of the national parties was able to raise and spend in the 1980 campaign is relevant. In hard money, the Republicans spent $64.6 million and the Democrats spent $13.9 million. The Republicans spent the full $4.6 million allocated for the Presidential account, while the Democrats have thus far reported spending $3.4 million. (Other costs the Democrats want to allocate to this account remained in dispute at the F.E.C., which was also investigating whether the Reagan campaign exceeded its spending limits.) William Brock, the Republican National Committee chairman from 1977 to 1981, went around the country emphasizing how important the money that the Party could spend on the Presidential campaign was, and he was so effective that he raised the amount that could be spent two or three times over. Thus, the Party had a great deal of money that it could put to other uses, such as television advertising—advertising that was ostensibly for the Party as a whole but, obviously, helped the Presidential candidate—and get-out-the-vote drives. The Republicans were so successful at raising both soft and hard money that the Reagan campaign was relieved of spending virtually any money for field organization in, for example, Texas—one of the most important and expensive states. Richard Wirthlin says, "One reason we were able to maximize our money in the Reagan campaign was that those kinds of questions had been considered by the Party a year and a half before the election. The field operation of our campaign is a side of the campaign that hasn't been told fully. Timmons had that down to a gnat's eyelash. There was no question in his mind or mine that we would deliver that vote." Of the total amount that can be raised via the various accounts, Timmons says, "You add all these things up and it's a pretty good hunk of change."

Thus, by conservative estimates, the Republican Party was able to spend directly—that is, not even counting Party expenditures at large—on behalf of its Presidential candidate: the $29.4 million in federal funds, the $4.6 million in hard money contributed by the national committee, the at least nine million dollars in soft money, and the money raised by the states. An additional amount was spent by "independent committees" on

Reagan's behalf—of which more later. The Democrats raised about $1.3 million in soft money and another two to four million altogether at the state level—or less than the Republicans are believed to have raised in Texas alone. Although it is often argued that the unions' get-out-the-vote drives are of great value, there is no way to put a price on them. In fact, all sorts of estimates float around as to how much money the Democrats and the Republicans spent respectively. And each side tends to exaggerate the amount that the other spent. But no one knows the exact numbers, because they are not reported in sum anywhere. So, in a system that is supposed to be equitable and measurable, no one really knows what is going on. The real point is that a path around the intent of the law has been found. And once such a path has been found it is usually widened. The problem is not the disparity itself so much as the fact that there is so much money in Presidential elections beyond what is allocated under the federal-financing law.

It is the amount of both hard and soft money that still goes to the election of a President—beyond the amount provided under the federal-financing scheme—that leads the former F.E.C. official to say that the idea that Presidential campaigns are no longer dependent on private money is a "fraud." Robert Keefe agrees. "No kidding" was his totally unsurprised reply when I suggested that this was the conclusion one reached after learning of all the rivers of private money that still flow into the Presidential campaign. It is this that leads Keefe to say, "They are overregulating the penguins on the tip of the iceberg."

There is actually a great deal that an individual who wants to give a lot of money to elect a President can do. Individuals may contribute up to twenty thousand dollars to a national committee, but this counts against their limit under the law for all federal contributions—the limit being ostensibly twenty-five thousand dollars for all candidates per two-year election cycle but in reality fifty thousand dollars for candidates and parties if the right moves are made. Both parties encourage large donations by offering special status and access to important people.

For ten thousand dollars a year, for instance, one can belong to the Eagles—a special Republican Party group. At one point in 1980, there were eight hundred and sixty-five Eagles. For five thousand dollars a year, one can belong to the Democratic Party's Finance Council. At its zenith in 1980, the Finance Council had about seven hundred members. The Democrats later established a Business Council, with a ten-thousand-dollar membership fee.

$$\boxed{15}$$

The Republican drive to raise soft money and channel it into the states in 1980 was thorough, and it was successful—and it enabled a number of people to give large amounts of unreported money. Nofziger says, "You won't find in the reports what individuals were doing to try to help elect Reagan."

I asked him if that meant that the F.E.C. reports showed only a piece of what is actually going on in a Presidential campaign.

"Oh, sure," he replied.

When several people who knew about the Republican drive for untraceable, unreported soft money in 1980 were asked for the names of those who were most generous, some familiar names emerged. The drive was headed by Ted Welch, of Nashville, Tennessee, an investor and a former finance chairman of the Republican National Committee—"one of the greatest fund raisers in America," Perkins says—and Robert Mosbacher, a Houston oil and gas producer, who had been George Bush's finance chairman during Bush's campaign for the Presidential nomination. Among those who were most valuable in helping the Reagan campaign raise soft money were Charles Wick and his wife, Mary Jane. The Wicks and the Reagans had been close friends in California. "Wick was really the honcho of the whole thing," one Republican I talked to said. Wick, who became the director of the International Communication Agency, is a former booking agent for bands who made a fortune in nursing homes (he also co-produced the movie "Snow White and the Three Stooges"). Wick and his wife not only contributed money themselves but also raised money from others whose names and financial generosity have been associated with Reagan's political career from the outset: Justin Dart, of Dart & Kraft, Inc. (formerly Dart Industries) and Holmes Tuttle, a Los Angeles automobile dealer. One person who was close to this enterprise says, "Charlie Wick went out and raised a lot of money for the Republican National Committee. I wouldn't be surprised if it wasn't more than two million bucks. The Wicks held parties and all kinds of events—and one thing and another." (Wick declined to answer questions on this subject.)

Joseph Coors, a familiar name among donors to right-wing causes, has also been cited as a donor to the Republican soft-money campaign. Among the others who are said to have been major benefactors is David Murdock, a Los Angeles builder, who is the largest stockholder in Occidental Petroleum and owns Cannon Mills. A great deal of soft money was raised in Texas, especially from people in the oil industry. One contributor was H. E. (Eddie) Chiles, of Fort Worth, who is chairman of the board of a large oil-field-services firm and is famous in the Southwest for doing his own radio ads, saying "I'm mad"— usually at the federal bureaucracy for one outrage or another. Chiles is also well known in political circles for funding conservative candidates. Another was James Lyon, a Houston banker who had been Reagan's finance chairman for Texas in 1976 and whom few Republican candidates fail to court. Perkins says, "Twenty or thirty percent of the money came out of Texas, and Oklahoma and Kansas were very helpful, too. You talk less about state lines than areas of influence. The area of influence in Texas and Oklahoma and Kansas is the oil business." Most of the money, Perkins says, "came from people who are first-generation rich—oil people, entrepreneurs." He adds, "All the Republican committees are successful at raising from them; they want to preserve the system that made them successful." It was this segment of the oil industry that also poured a lot of money into the Republican efforts to unseat Democratic incumbents in the House and Senate in 1980. And it is this same group that some

Democrats, in their desperation for money, tried to woo by offering tax breaks in 1981, thus setting off the "bidding war" over that year's tax-cut bill.

Perkins says that donors were asked to give twenty-five thousand dollars, and that the donations ranged from ten thousand to fifty thousand dollars. "What we asked for was whatever we could get," Perkins says. The donors were told which states to send their money to. In order to reward people who contributed, and tempt others to contribute, the Reagans gave a party in late October at Wexford, the house in rural Virginia where they were staying. Perkins remembers the evening well, because on the previous day a fall storm had blown down the tent in which the dinner was to be held, and everyone ended up inside the Reagans' house. "Obviously, the party was a good recruitment technique," Perkins says. "The general plan for the party was that the people there had already given, but that doesn't mean some weren't asked for more." Besides the Reagans, various campaign officials were present, and gave little pep talks. Timmons recalls, "All of us were paraded out there before these heavy hitters." This was actually the second event that the Reagans held at Wexford for large contributors. In September, they had a party there for Eagles—and potential Eagles.

Contributors were also given opportunities to show their regard for the Reagan Administration after the election. A separate fund, called the Transition Foundation, was established to help pay for the costs of the transition—contributors were asked to give five thousand dollars. Then yet another organization, this one called the Presidential Inaugural Committee, which established an Inaugural Trust Fund, was formed by Charles Wick and Robert Gray, the public-relations executive, to contribute funds to help pay for the Inauguration. The government pays two million dollars for the transition, and covers only a small part of the cost of the Inauguration. These "foundations" accepted corporate and personal contributions of as much as thirty thousand dollars. A former Reagan campaign official says, "That's when you can really go to town. Of course everyone wants to buy in with the new President." The Inauguration was both the most splendid in the history of the country and the most expensive—it cost over sixteen million dollars. Gray said, "This was free enterprise at its best."

Early in 1981, the still enthusiastic and energetic Wick set out to establish a committee—the Coalition for a New Beginning—that would accept funds from private contributors to help get the President's economic program passed. Wick and Justin Dart, another enthusiastic backer of the project, had the idea that corporations should contribute fifty thousand dollars each. Corporations, and their chief executives, of course, stood to gain from the President's program. Some eight hundred thousand dollars had rolled in by the end of March, but by then the project had become such an embarrassment that White House aides forced it to shut down. Wick and Dart were said to have been a bit heavy-handed in their techniques; a White House aide said that Wick had told businessmen that if they didn't come up with the fifty thousand dollars the Administration wouldn't be their friend. The Reagan White House people finally decided that this whole approach lacked subtlety—projecting as it did the image of the rich getting together to back a program that would be of particular help to them. One Reagan adviser says, "Those are things you would rather do quietly."

Many people from Texas and Oklahoma who had been so helpful in the Republican soft-money drive in 1980 also turned up, along with the Reagans' California friends, on the list of benefactors who had contributed to the Reagans' redecoration of the White House in 1981. The project's announced goal had been two hundred thousand dollars, but such was the interest in contributing to this fund that it amassed over eight hundred thousand dollars. (The contributions were tax-deductible.) This drive, which was headed by Holmes Tuttle, was ended after it became known that twenty-three of its contributors with oil interests had given a total of two hundred and seventy thousand dollars within weeks after Reagan speeded up the phased decontrol of oil prices. Tuttle had given parties in Oklahoma City and Houston to appeal for contributions. Contributors were asked to give ten thousand dollars apiece. Also on the list were a number of the Reagans' close friends, including Justin Dart, Alfred Bloomingdale, a founder of Diners' Club, Earle Jorgensen, a steel magnate, and Tuttle. And the George Bushes were helped out in the redecoration of the Vice-Presidential mansion by a group of wealthy Texans. That drive was headed by Earle Craig, an oil producer and a friend of Bush's, who said that though he would ask for contributions of ten thousand dollars each, there were no limits on how many members of a family could contribute that amount. He said he had solicited members of his own family, who, he was quoted as saying, "wouldn't be where they are today if it weren't for Uncle Earle."

Members of Reagan's "kitchen cabinet"—Dart, Tuttle, Jorgensen, and others—installed themselves in offices in the Old Executive Office Building, next to the White House, after the Inauguration and stayed there until some White House aides, disturbed about the propriety, and even the legality, of this, got them evicted. The kitchen cabinet had already played a large role in selecting the members of the Reagan Cabinet and other officials. Reagan advisers are wont to say that these people did not play a significant financial role in the campaign, because of the public-financing system. Now it is clear that they were in a position to be of great help. Because of the streams of unreported money, the contributions of these people can never be fully known, but even from the reports at the Federal Election Commission it is clear that several longtime Reagan backers contributed heavily to the 1980 elections. Not all the money went to the Reagan primary campaign or to the Republican National Committee; some of it also went to "independent committees" that were working on Reagan's behalf, and some went to other conservative candidates. And none of the following summaries of how much some large givers contributed take into account the unreported soft money they donated.

In all, the extended Coors family put into the 1980 elections almost a hundred and fifty thousand dollars in money reported at the federal level—over four thousand of it to Reagan, and the rest to various Republican committees, to the Coors brewing company's own political-action committee, and to such groups as the Committee for the Survival of a Free Congress and the Moral Majority. Joseph Coors and his wife, Holly, together contributed over eighty thousand dollars in reported sums, and their two sons contributed thirty-five thousand dollars; the Coors committee contributed a hundred and nineteen thousand dollars—three thousand to Reagan, and almost all the rest to conservative Republican candidates for the House and Senate. The Holmes Tuttles contributed nineteen thousand dollars in reported money—a thousand each directly to Reagan (the maximum), and four thousand to the Dart & Kraft political-action committee. Justin Dart and his wife, Jane, gave almost fifty thousand dollars in reported contributions. Each gave Reagan a thousand dollars, and together they gave twenty thousand dollars to the Dart & Kraft PAC, which, in turn, gave over three thousand dollars to Reagan. But the Dart & Kraft PAC appeared to take out some insurance: it gave three thousand dollars to Carter. In all, the Dart & Kraft PAC, one of the top contributors in 1980, gave out two hundred and forty-one thousand dollars, most of it to conservative Republicans but some to strategic Democrats. Among these were Dan Rostenkowski, the chairman of the House Ways and Means Committee; Elliott Levitas, the Georgia Democrat, who is the sponsor of legislation to allow Congress to override rulings of the federal regulatory agencies; Richard Gephardt, the Democrat from Missouri, who is an influential young member of the Ways and Means Committee; and Thomas Foley, the Democrat from Washington and the House Majority Whip. Dart also gave another five thousand dollars to the Republican National Committee after the general election.

The Democrats, distracted by the Carter-Kennedy struggle for the nomination, didn't consider the soft-money matter until late in the game, and didn't raise very much by that method. Most of the Democrats' soft money—the $1.3 million raised at the national level and the three to four million at the state level—came from the unions. Toward the end of the campaign, Robert Strauss, then the chairman of the Carter-Mondale reelection campaign, put a great deal of energy into raising soft money from labor and also from some of his wealthy connections. Actually, since there is no record, no one is quite sure how much the Democrats raised in soft money. Robert Keefe says, "Even those of us who were involved can't tell you exactly how much." The Democrats were having trouble raising money for their federal accounts—hard money—as well. Keefe told me, "I call hard money 'hard' because it's hard to raise." He added, "We had what we called hard, soft, and squishy money. Most federal or state laws require that you account for where the money comes from. You can't always do that. 'Squishy' is what you can't account for. If a ten-thousand-dollar cash contribution comes in from a fund-raising event in Chicago, you don't know who the hell it came from." The squishy money, Keefe said, was put into states—for example, Illinois—that allowed cash transactions. The other help that the Democrats could get was from the unions' own activities—which weren't notably successful at delivering the vote in 1980—and from nonprofit voter-education groups, such as Operation Big Vote, which registered blacks, and the Southwest Voter Registration Project, which registered Hispanics.

So the Presidential campaign is not free of the race for money, or of the influence of private money and interests. Some think that it may be only a matter of time before some Presidential nominee who has access to large amounts of money simply forgoes the federal contribution altogether, and thus frees himself from any limits on spending. (He would still be subject to the limits on contributions.) But, given what has already been discovered about how to raise private money in addition to the federal funds, that might not be necessary.

The big contributor or effective fund raiser is not forgotten, of course, if his candidate gets into the White House. One former Carter White House aide says, "You'll try to do a favor for someone you know to be a big fund raiser." Another says, "Clearly, if a big fund raiser wanted attention he got it. Unless it would get us in big trouble, we'd try to do what he wanted." The rewards of having helped the successful candidate at the right moment and to the right extent go beyond that. This former Carter White House aide says, "People making policy in the other parts of the executive branch, as well as in the White House, are sensitive to the fund raisers." And if the help was provided by a group—a union, for example—the kindness will be repaid, if possible. The Carter White House pushed for a separate Department of Education—which many people felt was a bad idea—because of the important help that the National Education Association had provided in 1976. The help provided by the maritime unions in 1976 led the Carter Administration to back legislation requiring that a certain percentage of imported oil be transported on (more expensive) American ships. Only an attack on this by the Republicans, and publicity about it in the press, led to the proposal's defeat. Carter, it may be recalled, had campaigned on the theme "I owe the special interests nothing."

16

To determine how an individual could have a big money-raising role in a Presidential campaign despite the restrictions, I constructed a hypothetical person named Fred and asked political advisers in both parties what Fred could do. Said a Democratic aide who has been involved in Presidential campaigns, "Fred is someone with a corporation, and identity in his community, and a variety of interests. He might live in New York, Chicago, L.A.—or a number of places." Fred, this man explained, could give the candidate for the nomination the maximum of a thousand dollars, and so could his wife and children, and so could his mother and father, his in-laws, his brother, his brother's wife, and on and on. (The rules are vague on how old children have to be to be deemed potential contributors; under F.E.C. rulings, the money has to be the children's own, and they have to be of a "sufficient age"—otherwise undefined—to have "donative intent." A donation by a three-year-old would raise questions.) If the fund raiser's children were married, their spouses could contribute. "There are a lot of big families around," the Democratic aide said. Then—and this is where Fred can be especially valuable—he could reach out to business associates, to high-level employees, to subcontractors. The aide said, "When Fred goes through his executives, his suppliers, his vendors, his subcontractors, his customers, maybe even his landlord—Fred might be the largest tenant—you've got somebody with economic reach." He continued, "Fred can host a number of events for a candidate, to introduce him to his friends and business associates. That's not unimportant. But, better yet, he'll just get on the phone for a day and call them up and ask them to contribute." Moreover, many states, such as Texas, allow contributions to people running for delegate to the national Convention. So a contributor who has done his all for the candidate can also give to someone running for delegate who is pledged to support that candidate at the Convention.

Then, once a candidate is nominated, the contributor can give twenty thousand dollars to the national party and unlimited sums to the soft-money state-party account. Thus, despite the fact that there is now a system of federal financing for Presidential campaigns, Fred can still be a big man—one whom the candidate will court and listen to—because of both what he can contribute and what he can raise from others. As early as three years before the 1984 election, all over America potential Presidential candidates were auditioning before Fred and his friends. If a candidate for the nomination believes he has enough contributors and fund raisers behind him, he might decide—as Connally did in 1980—to forgo the federal financing, with its spending limits. One major Democratic fund raiser remarked in the fall of 1982, "If we had a really hot one for a Presidential candidate in 1984, we wouldn't worry about federal money." One former Reagan campaign official said, "Fred, if he's a savvy guy, can leverage his ability to raise money and become a very important person. The possibilities are infinite." When I presented my "Fred" question to another man closely involved in the 1980 Reagan campaign, he replied without hesitation, "Ray Donovan is Fred."

Raymond Donovan, the Secretary of Labor, had been a star fund raiser for Reagan. He was the classic right man at the right place at the right time—and he made a smart move. Another former Reagan campaign official said, "The reason Ray Donovan is Secretary of Labor is that he was virtually the only heavy hitter in the Northeast who was raising money for Reagan between 1978 and 1980."

Donovan, then an official of the Schiavone Construction

Company, in Secaucus, New Jersey, had raised some money for James Buckley's Senate races in New York in 1970 and 1976. Beginning in 1979, according to Reagan campaign officials, Donovan set out early to raise a great deal of money for Reagan: he contributed, he got his friends to contribute, he got his company's subcontractors to contribute. How it goes, one Reagan campaign official says, is "Joe, can you give me two thousand—one from you and one from your wife—and can you raise me four?" And he adds, "The myth is that there is a limit. There really is not. You can't ask too many people; you can't ask too many times. If Joe Smith in Houston has given his federal limit, he can ask his brother-in-law." According to a campaign official, "In the period between the Iowa caucuses and the New Hampshire primary, when Reagan was really strapped for funds, Donovan was out there raising money like a bandit. And he came to the attention of Ronald and Nancy Reagan because he raised more than any other individual." It is estimated that Donovan raised at least six hundred thousand dollars for the Reagan campaign. Donovan, who became finance chairman of the Reagan New Jersey campaign, had the Reagans attend a fund-raiser at his country club, Fiddler's Elbow, in Bedminster, New Jersey, in September, 1979. The Reagans brought along Frank Sinatra for the occasion. Officials of Donovan's firm were responsible for selling half the tickets to the event, which raised an estimated hundred and sixty thousand dollars. In 1980, Donovan co-hosted another event for large contributors–fund raisers, at the Meadowlands, in New Jersey, with Sonny Werblin, the president of the Madison Square Garden Corporation. "Donovan tried to spend a lot of time with the candidate and his wife," a Reagan campaign official says. "That's a good way to get a Cabinet job." Leon Silverman, who was appointed a Special Prosecutor in 1982 to investigate allegations that Donovan had had links to organized-crime members—but found "insufficient credible evidence" to prosecute—referred some questions about Donovan's fund-raising methods to the Federal Election Commission. Among the allegations the F.E.C.

was understood to be investigating are that Donovan's aides used coercion on his company's employees and subcontractors, and that the use of employees to solicit funds may have violated federal prohibitions against direct or indirect corporate contributions. According to the Special Prosecutor's report, an official of Donovan's company was heard on an F.B.I. wiretap of an alleged organized-crime figure in June, 1979, saying that Reagan would be visiting Donovan soon, and that Donovan and his associates wished to "give this guy here, you know, a wad . . . green."

Donovan told people during the campaign that he wanted to be either Secretary of Labor or Ambassador to Ireland. After Donovan got the Cabinet post, the Reagan Administration's first choice for Ambassador to Ireland was, as it happens, William McCann, a New Jersey insurance executive, whom Donovan had got involved in fund-raising for Reagan. But then a rivalry had developed between the two men. When McCann started trying to obtain the Ambassadorship, Donovan called the White House to try to put a stop to it. After McCann was selected for the post, it was found that his firm's business practices were under investigation and that one of his close business associates was a convicted swindler and allegedly had ties to organized crime. The plans to nominate McCann were dropped.

Other major fund raiser–contributors did succeed in obtaining ambassadorships. Maxwell Rabb, named Ambassador to Italy, was an early fund raiser for Reagan. Rabb, a former secretary to the Cabinet in the Eisenhower Administration and a New York lawyer, raised a lot of money for Reagan in 1979 and 1980, when this was not fashionable—"smart money" in New York was on Connally or Bush—and he had the credentials to go to others in New York and get them to raise money for Reagan, too. Rabb was helpful in raising soft money for the state campaign as well. John J. Louis, named Ambassador to Great Britain, had tried to obtain this post from Richard Nixon, having contributed to his campaigns. In 1969, Louis, an heir to the Johnson Wax fortune, had lost out to Walter Annenberg, the wealthy publisher. In 1968, contributions did not have to be reported, but in 1972 Louis gave nearly three hundred thousand dollars to Nixon's reelection campaign. (Annenberg contributed a quarter of a million dollars to Nixon's reelection campaign in 1972.) Louis continued to be disappointed, as Gerald Ford named Elliot Richardson and then Anne Armstrong to the post after Annenberg left it. In the 1980 election, Louis covered his bets by giving contributions to Reagan, Bush, and Connally. These were subject to the thousand-dollar limit, but Louis and his wife also gave large sums to the Republican National Committee and related groups. Louis says he really can't remember when he might have made what contributions to Reagan's election. By this time, Mr. and Mrs. Louis had become friendly with the Annenbergs, and Louis says, "It occurred to Mr. Annenberg and a couple of his other friends that maybe I, John Louis, might go into public service." So Louis and his wife were invited by the Annenbergs to spend the New Year's holiday at the end of 1980 with, among others, the Reagans at the Annenbergs' home in Palm Springs. The day after Louis left, Reagan called him and offered him the post of Ambassador to the Court of St. James's.

John Loeb, Jr., appointed Ambassador to Denmark, was also helpful to the Reagan campaign. He gave a thousand dollars to Reagan and twenty-five hundred to one of the "independent committees" that were formed on Reagan's behalf, and, more important, he helped raise money for Reagan in New York. Yet the major reason for Loeb's getting the ambassadorship, according to Reagan sources, was that he had curried favor with such people as Dart and Tuttle. Helene von Damm, Reagan's executive assistant, had the role of seeing that the Reagan supporters got government jobs. (Miss von Damm was later made head of the personnel office, and in 1983 was named Ambassador to Austria.) Miss von Damm is said to have been indignant over Loeb's appointment; she felt that he had not raised enough money to earn it, in comparison with, say, Donovan. Other ambassadorial appointments also went to men whose only credentials appeared to be that they had been financially helpful to the

Reagan effort. (The Carter Administration awarded a few ambassadorships to people who had raised substantial funds, but not to the extent the Reagan Administration did.) John Shad, a former investment banker and a director of E. F. Hutton, raised a lot of money for Reagan on Wall Street. He is now the chairman of the Securities and Exchange Commission.

Each party has its own itinerary for seeking out the fund raisers. (Senatorial candidates follow much the same routes as Presidential ones.) And while the person who is individually wealthy and gathers his wealthy friends—the "Malibu liberals," for example, for the Democrats—is valuable, the businessman with an extensive business network is even more valuable. A former Carter Administration official says, "If you want a hundred people to come up with a thousand dollars, you have to have a businessman who can hit up his suppliers and business cronies." Moreover, certain fund raisers consider themselves the *sine qua non* in their areas. Says the former official, "The fund-raising structure is not unlike the Mafia. If you want to do business in that area, there is one person you have to deal with." If the big donors don't want to commit themselves early to a particular candidate, lesser lights are sought out in the meantime. The former Carter aide says that Lew Wasserman, the chairman and chief executive officer of MCA and the kingpin of Democratic fund-raising in Los Angeles, "put Carter in a box" in 1980. He says, "If Wasserman doesn't return your phone calls, you can't do business in Los Angeles. Wasserman will put you through Chinese water torture before he'll raise money for you, and he won't let anyone else do it." Among other things, Wasserman was reportedly irritated with Carter for not coming to his house, and he also wanted to be in charge of fund-raising. Eventually Wasserman relented and raised money for Carter. Steven Ross, the chairman of Warner Communications, has been considered the most important Democratic fund raiser in New York, because of his company's large number of suppliers. Nathan Landow, a real-estate magnate in the Washington area, has become an important fund raiser. One Democrat says, "Nate is popular because he comes through. He just enjoys being the main guy in his area, and palling around with politicians."

The Democrats' route is New York, Los Angeles, San Francisco, Chicago, Miami, and—depending on the candidate—Texas. The Republicans' route has been changing, moving west, toward the new entrepreneurs, with the changing ideological balance in the Party. The Republican geographical shift, according to John Sears and others, began with Barry Goldwater. Sears says, "Since the Eastern interests didn't finance him, he had to go other places." The Republican candidate will still trek to New York, because there is so much money there, but a John Connally or a George Bush is more likely to raise money in New York than a Ronald Reagan. But whereas a Robert Taft or an Eisenhower went to New York, Chicago, and Boston, and contemporary candidates might buzz through these cities, the more rewarding stops now are Dallas, Houston, Tulsa, Los Angeles, and San Diego. Each candidate, of course, may have a particular strain he can tap. In 1980, George Bush did well with fellow Yale alumni, and, according to a Bush campaign aide, even used the mailing list for the J. Press catalogue. John Sears says, "The Democrats thought they were erasing the Republican advantage in money with the campaign-finance law putting limits on contributions, but if there are people with money they're going to surface. And there are more Lew Wassermans on the Republican side."

17

In recent years, potential but unannounced Presidential candidates have increasingly turned to yet another device for raising money beyond the limits of the public-financing law, and so furthering their ambitions: they establish their own political-action committees, whose funds they draw upon to make contributions to other politicians and to defray the expenses they incur while actually or ostensibly campaigning for candidates for the Senate and House, or state and local office. Even after they officially announce their candidacy, their PACS can still be used for some purposes. By November of 1982, Edward Kennedy, Walter Mondale, Ernest Hollings, Morris Udall, Robert Dole, Jack Kemp, and Howard Baker all had their own PACS. (Kennedy and Udall later announced that they would not run. And when Mondale announced that he would not take PAC money, it was also decided that he would close down his own PAC. Udall, who nurtured the dream that the 1984 Democratic Convention would be deadlocked, and turn to him, maintained his PAC.) Jesse Helms had had a PAC, the Congressional Club, for some time, which he used for a variety of purposes. For the potential nominee, using PAC money is a way of making an appearance on behalf of another candidate without the candidate's having to pay for it—of helping himself by helping others. The PAC can make an out-and-out contribution to another candidate—for which it is assumed he will be grateful when the race for the nomination is on. Since it is a PAC, it can make a contribution of five thousand dollars, rather than the one thousand dollars that can be contributed by an individual—and it can receive contributions of five thousand dollars, rather than one thousand, from individuals. Furthermore, it can set up a non-federal account to which soft money, with its lack of restrictions, can be contributed. The PAC's non-federal account can accept corporate money, union money, and unlimited personal contributions.

The justification for having a non-federal account is that the candidate can draw on it to go into a state to support a candidate for state or local office—for governor, state legislator, mayor, and so on. An aide to one potential Presidential candidate said, "There is no limit to what someone can give us in our non-federal account, and that's valuable to us. If there were a mayor's race or a governor's race where a state law permitted us to give a quarter of a million dollars—which in about half the states it does—I can't imagine we'd have any difficulty in getting their support for our race." He continued. "Someone called me this week and said, 'I'd like to help. What can I do?' I said, 'You can give five thousand dollars per person per year for your entire family to our federal account, and you can give an unlimited amount of money personally, or from any one of the corporations you control, to our non-federal account.' " The aide continued, "He asked what the limits were on what he could give, and I said, 'None.' "

Another possibility is that a person whose sole interest is a particular Presidential candidate can give that candidate's PAC five thousand dollars, and then gather money for candidates running for other offices and make it clear that the contribution is at the Presidential candidate's behest. The Presidential candidate and the donor can even show up together to deliver the check. "Obviously," an aide to one would-be candidate says, "that's a hell of an asset." Another way a Democratic candidate can help himself along is by having money given to his party through his PAC. He can also encourage a contributor to give to the Party's soft-money account, on which there is no limit. The candidate can then go to the Party chairman and suggest, for example, that he commission a poll that could help the candidate ascertain his chances—and he can even stipulate the pollster. The pollster may, amazingly, turn out to be one who is also working for the candidate. If the Party chairman is questioned about being so cooperative, he can simply shrug and say that he is giving the poll results to anyone who wants them. One political adviser says, "There are all sorts of situations within each party where people get a special privilege resulting from their financial assistance—tempered only by somebody screaming too loud."

Once a candidate has actually announced that he is seeking the nomination, he sets up his own fund-raising mechanism ("Citizens for Smith") and proceeds to raise money for it. From that point on, all his activities are presumed to be on behalf of his candidacy, and are charged to his official campaign. But he can also keep the PAC—at a distance—and this has some advantages. The rules on this are unclear, since it is a field in which people are pioneering. He cannot use the PAC for political activities on his own behalf, but he can use it to raise money for candidates for other offices and to continue to build a direct-mail list; in addition, if he should win the nomination the PAC's non-federal account can put soft money into states, to be used to get out the vote. Says an aide to one prospective Presidential candidate, "An awful lot of senators and congressmen will start to raise their reelection money in 1983, and they would probably appreciate a contribution from us."

The granddaddy of this kind of PAC was Ronald Reagan's Citizens for the Republic, which was started after Reagan's 1976 campaign, with the money and the mailing lists left over from that venture. It helped fund Reagan's activities until he became a declared candidate once again. (Connally and Bush had PACs before the 1980 campaign as well.) During Reagan's formal run for the Presidency in 1980, Citizens for the Republic contributed money to candidates for the House and Senate, and raised corporate funds, which it put into the state of California and elsewhere. The F.E.C. is investigating a complaint brought by the National Committee for an Effective Congress, a liberal group, that Citizens for the Republic made excessive contributions to the Reagan campaign for the nomination. Citizens for the Republic still exists, with an office in Santa Monica. Reagan is the chairman emeritus, and the present chairman is Lyn Nofziger, who advises Citizens for the Republic where to contribute its funds. Having the President on its letterhead is presumably helpful to its fund-raising. In 1982 it contributed four hundred and seventy thousand dollars to a hundred and fifteen candidates, all of them Republican, and an unknown amount in corporate money to state parties. A PAC with the President's name on it is a new twist, and raises new questions. Contributors receive a Distinguished Presidential Support Certificate, citing them "for steadfastly and generously supporting President Ronald Reagan through the political action committee he founded, Citizens for the Republic, during the historic political battles facing his Administration."

18

The changing patterns of fund-raising have also given rise to the phenomenon of direct-mail fund-raising—the implications and the uses of which are only dimly understood. The fact that Barry Goldwater could not raise money from established Republican sources led to the development of the "small contributor," and of mailing lists of such people. (It was Goldwater's 1964 lists that gave the Republican Party its start in direct-mail fund-raising.) A by-product of this changing pattern is that our politics have become more ideological. The more successful direct-mail drives are those that appeal to the emotions—particularly on such issues as gun control, abortion, school prayer, "big government," the environment, arms control, and Social Security. A candidate raises money on the basis of these issues, not on the argument that he is likely to govern well, be reasonable, or steer a safe and steady course. He is a vehicle for expressing those things people feel most strongly about. The direct-mail appeal is often couched in terms of an attack on the opposition and is frequently unfair. (Also, direct mail, unlike a television appeal, can be targeted at specific groups, and thus, by aiming different messages at different audiences, contributes to the splinterization of politics.) Any direct-mail expert will tell you that it is easier to raise money for an emotional issue than for a candidate unless the candidate is strongly identified with emotional issues. Therefore, it is axiomatic that as candidates try to raise money through direct mail—and more and more of them do—their appeals will have to be increasingly shrill. Moderation has not proved to be a good money raiser. Ronald Reagan did very well with direct mail; over the years, he built a base among those who felt strongly about the kinds of issues he stressed—"big government," the social issues. As direct mail moves candidates to the extremes, it reduces their flexibility, and it also makes it more difficult to reach consensus. One conservative political activist says, "It's easier to break a commitment to one contributor than to a hundred thousand contributors to whom you've committed yourself on paper." Jim Leach, the moderate Republican congressman from Iowa, says, "America, as a society, with all its diversity, functions by exercising tolerance. The fund-raising mail can be classified as intolerant, as stressing divisions, not healing them."

There have obviously been a number of ideological individual large contributors as well, whether they are Joseph Coors or Stewart Mott (the General Motors heir who gives large amounts to liberal causes), Justin Dart or a Malibu liberal. But in the past the big givers have tended by and large to be pragmatic. As the costs of campaigns have been allowed to rise, candidates have turned increasingly to direct mail as a source of funds. The big donor–fund raiser can still be of great help, but a direct-mail solicitation does not take the time of the candidate and his staff that a fund-raising dinner does.

The lists are developed by testing various pools—subscribers to certain journals, supporters of previous candidates, contributors to causes. The major cost is developing the lists, but once they are developed it is relatively inexpensive to go back and back to those contributors. The Republican Party says that it raises about seventy percent of its funds through direct mail. The Democrats, having been outdone on direct mail for many years, are now developing their lists—drawing on lists of those who gave to George McGovern or Morris Udall, and on lists of contributors to the environmental movement or to organizations opposed to restrictions on abortions. The Democratic Party's most successful direct-mail issue in 1982 was Social Security. The Democrats have a basic list of about two hundred thousand direct-mail contributors; the Republicans have a list of about a million seven hundred thousand.

The disparity between what the two parties can raise through direct mail is likely to continue, because of the different nature of their constituencies. For the most part, people who respond to the Democrats' direct-mail issues tend to be upper middle class. The poor and the blue-collar workers who make up the rest of the potential base either do not respond to such issues or do not have spare cash to contribute. An aide to one potential Presidential candidate says, "On the liberal side, there is a universe of about three million people who have been identified with anything liberal—McGovern, the environment, the abortion-rights movement, arms control, gun control—and they're upper middle class. Once you exhaust that, you get to the blue-collar worker, and not only don't those issues work with him but he doesn't have that much to give." Paul Dietrich, the president of the Fund for a Conservative Majority, says, "I don't think the Democrats will ever raise as much as we can, because we have very sophisticated marketing studies that tell us that our contributors are suburban and rural, and over fifty, and they tend to be very, very frustrated. They don't have any outlet for their political feelings. They tend not to be from New York, one of the most populous states, but from the South, the Southwest, and the West. Most of those people have good conservative congressmen, but there's not very much they feel they can do to turn the country around. They give to us because they know we'll go after 'those Easterners.' The Democrats' people tend to be more educated and more urban, and—other than those from California—more Eastern. They have other outlets for their political frustrations and energies. They can be precinct chairmen; you can't do that in a rural area. The more educated ones can go out and talk to their congressmen, go to a fund-raiser, have access to people with power—can voice their opinion. Our people are more frustrated. Our marketing studies confirm it. The Democrats will never be able to raise the money that we raise."

But the real point about direct mail, as about other forms of money-raising, is not how well one group or another does with it but what it does to the political system. What sort of candidates does it produce, and does it make it harder to govern? A number of people say that there is a fair amount of chicanery involved in direct mail. Because it is a relatively new business, and one in which the costs and the receipts are difficult to track, some direct-mail operators see it as a way of making easy money. Some, such as Richard Viguerie, on the right, and Roger Craver and Tom Mathews, who operate the most successful liberal direct-mail operation, have good reputations, but some others work under questionable arrangements. In addition, direct-mail operations can mislead their contributors. One conservative activist says, "There is great potential for fraud. There are organizations out there raising thousands and thousands of political dollars, and doing nothing like what they say they will do with the money." He singled out Jesse Helms' Congressional Club: "I know one conservative candidate who had to bleed for a thousand dollars from them. A lot of their money goes into their tremendous overhead—a large staff, computers, the whole works. What happens is little old ladies in Peoria are asked to give money to help national congressional campaigns, but an enormous amount of their money ends up going into Jesse's fight to maintain his power in North Carolina." Governor James Hunt, of North Carolina, a Democrat, is expected to oppose Helms for the Senate in 1984.

But not all direct mail is aimed at raising money; it is also a device for helping candidates by sending out propaganda on their behalf. Paul Dietrich says, "If I pump a hundred thousand pieces of mail into a candidate's district, and it has four pages about the candidate, and a tag line asking for money for the candidate—and it always does—I've helped that candidate by sending the letters and pumping him up. Then I turn around and give him five thousand dollars, which is all I'm legally allowed to do, and my letter is counted as a fund-raising appeal, not as a contribution. And then the press criticizes me for spending all my money on fund-raising, and not giving direct contributions to candidates. I sit there and laugh."

19

The 1980 election also gave rise to another major method of routing private money into a Presidential campaign—the so-called "independent committee." When an individual runs out of ways to help a Presidential candidate—though that might seem to be impossible—he can always turn to the device of the "independent" expenditure. The actual effect of independent expenditures by independent committees is to totally upend the intent of the law providing for public financing of Presidential campaigns: that the two candidates would run against each other on an equal financial basis, and that the only role for private money would be through the political parties—and that to a limited extent. The aim of the overwhelming proportion of independent expenditures by independent committees on the Presidential level in 1980 was to provide more money to help elect Reagan. Only about two million dollars was spent independently in 1976. In 1980, twelve million dollars was spent independently on Reagan's behalf, and forty-six thousand on Carter's. Much of the spending on Reagan's behalf was done by three already established ideological political-action committees—the Fund for a Conservative Majority, Jesse Helms' Congressional Club, and the National Conservative Political Action Committee (NCPAC). But a great deal of it was done by two groups specially created for the exercise.

The independent committees developed as a phenomenon in Presidential elections following the Supreme Court decision in *Buckley v. Valeo*, in January of 1976, which held that the 1974 federal election law's prohibition of independent spending of more than a thousand dollars on any election by individuals or groups was a violation of the First Amendment's guarantee of freedom of speech. Having thus struck down this broad provision—and, in effect, equated freedom of speech with spending money—the Court opened up another route by which private money could travel into a Presidential campaign. The Court said that such independent expenditures did not, in its words, "presently appear" to pose any problems. This was an easy enough observation to make: at the time the Court ruled, there were no independent expenditures on Presidential campaigns. The Buckley suit (Buckley was James Buckley, then a Conservative senator from New York) was brought by a coalition that included Eugene McCarthy, who was opposed to the public-financing law; the New York Civil Liberties Union; Stewart Mott; and the right-wing periodical *Human Events*—a coalition that had a variety of concerns about the federal campaign law and a variety of motives for wanting it struck down. The case was put together by David Keene, a young libertarian who initially worked for Buckley and then, in 1976, for Reagan; in 1980 he worked for George Bush and then for NCPAC. This suit was a general onslaught on the law, but the Court upheld the basic provisions: setting limits on how much individuals and political-action committees could contribute to candidates; establishing public financing of Presidential campaigns; and requiring disclosure of campaign contributions and expenditures. (The Court did, however, strike down any limit on what an individual could spend on his own campaign.) In 1976, Congress passed a new law to deal with some of the technical difficulties raised by the Court decision. (For a while during the 1976 primary period, there was no Federal Election Commission to distribute funds to candidates, because the Court had ruled against the way commission members were selected.) President Ford signed the law only reluctantly, having been under pressure to veto it from conservatives, business lobbyists, and Ronald Reagan. In order to narrow the opening left by the striking down of limits on independent expenditures, Congress required that individuals and committees making independent expenditures of more than a hundred dollars swear that the expenditures were not made in collusion with the candidate on whose behalf they were made. The prohibition is fairly vague, and is essentially beside the point. There are all manner of ways in which people running "independent" campaigns can run them in tandem with the candidates, and there are all manner of ways in which—without the candidate or his top aides necessarily getting involved—the independent committees and the campaigns can, and do, collude.

The kinds of things an independent committee would need to know in order to be effective are poll data indicating areas of weakness, the official campaign organization's plans for "media buys," and what themes to stress. Much of this can be found out by carefully reading the newspapers, but there are other ways as well. In fact, some information is deliberately planted in newspapers and newsletters so that those who are trying to be helpful can see it. Jesse Helms, whose Congressional Club made a four-and-a-half-million-dollar contribution on behalf of the Reagan campaign in 1980, was asked at the 1980 Republican Convention whether he had had any recent conversations with Reagan. He replied, "Well, as you may know, we have had an independent effort going on in North Carolina. The law forbids me to consult with him, and it's been an awkward situation. I've had to, sort of, talk indirectly with Paul Laxalt"—Reagan's campaign chairman—"and hope that he would pass along, uh, and I think the messages have got through all right." Paul Dietrich, whose Fund for a Conservative Majority spent two million dollars helping Reagan in both the primary and the general election, told me, "There is no way to enforce independence as long as there is a press corps giving us information and as long as one group puts out information and gets it to the others." For an independent committee to get involved in a primary is unusual, but all three of the existing ideological PACs that spent on Reagan's behalf in the general election also made efforts to help him win the primaries. When Reagan's campaign had nearly run out of money in the early primary period, the Fund for a Conservative Majority bought television time for Reagan in New Hampshire. NCPAC made a timely infusion of funds on Reagan's behalf during the late primaries, and Helms' Congressional Club spent for Reagan during the primaries. Two newsletters that are closely followed for such information are Kevin Phillips' *American Political Report* and Alan Baron's *Baron Report*. Reporters are also counted upon, and used, as bearers of useful gossip. But there are more direct methods of passing on relevant information. Says Dietrich, whose committee also works on senatorial and congressional elections, "If I really want a poll from the Republican National Committee or a campaign, I can get it. They'll leak it to me."

Leaking polls is apparently a fairly common phenomenon. If a national party gives a candidate the results of a poll in time for them to be of any use, this is counted as a contribution. But, says one conservative activist, "there's nothing they can do about a staff member who goes home with the information in his head and calls a reporter. Everyone winks when the staff calls the candidate at night and gives him the information."

I asked Lyn Nofziger how an independent committee in 1980 might have found out where it could be most helpful to the official campaign (where Reagan's strength needed shoring up, say, or where there might suddenly be an opening).

Nofziger replied, "I'd know through the polls that were available. I wouldn't have to talk to Bill Casey"—the director of the Reagan campaign. "I'd have a friend of mine talk to Bill Casey. I wouldn't have any problem getting that done. There's no way in the world that if I'm running an independent campaign I'm not going to get the information I need, or get Dick Wirthlin's data, or talk to the chairman of the national committee, or whatever. What can't happen is the chairman of the Republican National Committee coming to me and saying 'Can you do that?' and I can't say 'Should we do this?' But there are a lot of other conversations that can be held." As for coordinating media expenditures, Nofziger explained, "If the TV stations were selling me time, I could find out when the campaign was buying time." He added, "And I could go on the attack in a way that the campaign might not be comfortable doing." The negative attack by an independent committee working on a Presidential candidate's behalf can be an embarrassment; on the other hand, the candidate's campaign people can always try to shrug off the attack as something that was done by a bunch of people over whom they have no control—all the while gaining the benefits of the attack.

Roger Stone, a Republican political consultant who worked in the Reagan campaign, says, "You wouldn't have to be a genius to figure out where to spend the money. If Reagan suddenly shows up in Tennessee and Kentucky, you know that the campaign considers them winnable states. Or if the Vice-President, the Party chairman, and other key figures start trouping to Kentucky, you gather that Kentucky is winnable." Moreover, if an independent committee is conducting a poll on a Senate candidate in Illinois it may also learn something of value about the Presidential race.

As a matter of fact, there is a web of pollsters and consultants on each side of the political spectrum—a small community—whose information intertwines. There are only four major pollsters for the Republicans, three major media-consultant companies, and a very few general consultants. In any campaign year, these people are working for a number of candidates and committees. Stone says, "If you're plugged in to the political community, you can find out what's going on virtually everywhere." A Democratic consultant says, "The connections are so great it's almost like an organism." One pollster, Arthur Finkelstein, did some work for the Fund for a Conservative Majority and for the Reagan primary campaign, and has also served as a consultant to Helms. Richard Viguerie's organization, the largest of the right-wing direct-mail houses, did work for the Fund for a Conservative Majority, for Helms' organization, for NCPAC, and for the Reagan primary campaign. (An argument made by critics of this whole procedure was that pollsters and consultants who worked directly for the Reagan organization in the primaries and for the independent committees in effect never really left the Reagan campaign.) The same direct-mail lists are used by numerous groups.

Such interlocking also occurs between independent committees and the congressional campaigns on whose behalf they are working. A Republican consultant says, "There have been cases I know of where Individual X is hired by the senatorial campaign committee to do a poll for someone running for the Senate, and X is also a consultant for a certain independent political-action committee, advising it on how to use its funds in that particular state." He added, "I think that's a breach of the spirit, if not the letter, of the law—but it happens." Another political consultant says, "The way you can get messages back and forth is through the national committee, or the Senate or House campaign committee. The committee person would say, 'You understand I have nothing to do with your campaign, but it would seem to me it would make sense for you to do the following.' " Patrick Caddell, the Democratic pollster, says, "The principals in a campaign may never speak, but through reading the press and other things they can know as well as if they were sitting in the same room what states are being stressed, where you need help, where you don't want it, what your issues are. NCPAC went into the South and ran a very negative campaign against Carter, and said at the same time that these were states that Reagan was not concentrating on. I believe there was direct collusion among the Republicans, but you don't have to have it to make it work. Indirect collusion will work just fine if you have professional people who can read and write. Either they were colluding directly or the indirect collusion was enormous. Either way, the purpose of the law was defeated."

Two groups were established in 1980 specifically to raise and spend money on behalf of the Reagan campaign. David Keene says, "They were really formed to put the big money in." One group, Americans for Change, was headed by Senator Harrison Schmitt, Republican of New Mexico. (He was defeated in 1982.)

It called its project "Reagan for President in '80," and in its literature it described itself as a vehicle for raising money to elect Reagan. ("If you want to see a change in this nation in 1980 it's going to take much more than the $29 million that the federal government is allowing Ronald Reagan.") Other officials of Americans for Change had been connected with the Reagan campaign: James Edwards, the future Secretary of Energy, who had also served on the Republican National Committee's Advisory Council on Natural Resources and was a Reagan delegate to the 1980 Republican Convention; and Anna Chennault, who was an organizer of the Schmitt group at the same time that she was co-chairman of the Nationalities Division of the Reagan for President Committee and a member of the Republican National Committee's Advisory Committee on Fiscal Affairs. Americans for Change still exists, and the mailing lists it developed through its campaign for Reagan were made available to other candidates in 1982. Americans for Change is run by Brad O'Leary, a professional Republican fund raiser who in 1982 helped Schmitt, among others.

The other group established specifically to raise money on behalf of the Reagan campaign was Americans for an Effective Presidency. This group's aim was to gather funds from establishment Republicans. It was headed by Peter Flanigan, a former Nixon Administration official, who later became a managing director of the New York investment house of Dillon Read. Also among its officials was Thomas Reed, who had managed Reagan's 1970 gubernatorial campaign and later joined the Reagan National Security Council staff. (He resigned after charges of misuse of stock options.) William Clements, who served as chairman of the official Reagan campaign in Texas, was involved in the organization of Americans for an Effective Presidency, and was also a member of a Republican National Committee advisory committee. Actually, Stuart Spencer, a California political consultant who also had long been associated with Reagan campaigns, almost became the head of Americans for an Effective Presidency, but it was decided that there would be a problem of appearances. As one current Reagan aide put it, "he was too close to us." So Spencer was brought directly into the campaign. The fact that the Reagan people were even considering such a question suggests how un-independent the whole exercise was. The group's advertising was handled by Bailey, Deardourff & Associates, which had produced the advertising for the Ford campaign in 1976, and which ordinarily works for moderate Republicans.

There was, among all these groups and the Reagan campaign, simply an overall pattern of professional associations and interlocking relationships which subsumed all the individual threads. The details are less important than the obvious point that the intention of these groups was to amass large sums of private money to elect Reagan. Their efforts were directed toward complementing the Reagan campaign. And all parties concerned clearly knew what was going on. Americans for an Effective Presidency spent $1.3 million on behalf of the Reagan campaign, and Americans for Change spent a little over seven hundred thousand dollars. The committees had planned to raise and spend far more, but, one Republican activist says, potential contributors to these groups got "scared off" by suits challenging their legality. Both groups ran ads on behalf of Reagan, as did the Congressional Club, NCPAC, and the Fund for a Conservative Majority. The Congressional Club's literature said, "As an independent campaign, Americans for Reagan can spend an unlimited amount of money on behalf of Ronald Reagan." Helms' group called its activities "Americans for Reagan"; NCPAC called its "The Ronald Reagan Victory Fund"; the Fund for a Conservative Majority called its "Citizens for Reagan in '80." NCPAC's expenditures for Reagan came to nearly two million dollars, and the Fund for a Conservative Majority's to a little over two million dollars. Its literature said, "As an independent effort 'Citizens for Reagan in '80' has no limit on expenditures before or after the nomination," and "Ronald Reagan Needs You to Support 'Citizens for Reagan in '80' if He Is to Be Elected President."

Thus, the twelve million dollars that independent commit-tees spent for Reagan came to almost half as much as the twenty-nine million in federal financing. This was on top of the at least nine million dollars in soft money that was spent through state accounts, plus the $4.6 million in hard money spent by the Republican Party for the Presidential campaign directly (a very conservative figure, since a good bit of the rest of the $64.5 million in hard money spent by the Party helped Reagan as well), for a total of almost twenty-six million dol-lars—not even counting what was raised and spent by the state parties themselves. Therefore, far more private money than pub-lic funds went into Reagan's Presidential campaign. The total amount of extra private money spent for Carter was five million dollars ($3.4 million in hard money and $1.6 million in soft money), or one-fifth of what was spent for Reagan. (This doesn't count the rest of the Democratic National Committee's $13.9 million—about one-fifth of what the Republicans spent—or the two to four million that the Democrats raised in the states.) Thus, even by a conservative count, Reagan's advantage over Carter in funds was greater than Nixon's over Humphrey in 1968, and almost as great as Nixon's over McGovern in 1972. Again, the point is not that Reagan was elected because of money. The point is that the intent of the public-financing law has been destroyed. And in a Presidential contest where other things are more nearly equal, a candidate's ability to generate private money could still make the difference. Given history, it is clear that attempts to affect the course of the Presidential campaign by private money will grow.

In July of 1980, Common Cause sued Harrison Schmitt's group, charging collusion and again raising the question of in-dependent expenditures. The four other independent commit-tees working on Reagan's behalf were co-defendants. For one thing, the Supreme Court had said in the Buckley decision that independent committees did not at that point appear to present any problems. For another, the Buckley plaintiffs had over-looked a section of the law which placed a limit of a thousand

dollars on independent expenditures in connection with a publicly financed campaign, so this section was still on the books.
A lower court held that this provision, too, was unconstitutional, and that the question of collusion should be raised with
the Federal Election Commission. The constitutionality question was then taken to the Supreme Court, which, in January of
1982, split, four to four, and therefore did not rule on it. The
justice who did not participate in the case was Sandra Day
O'Connor, Reagan's first appointee to the Court. Mrs. O'Connor's recusing herself had been a mystery to the plaintiffs, and
was a disappointment to the defendants, who thought she
would rule on their side. As it happens, Mrs. O'Connor's husband, an Arizona attorney, had served on the Finance Committee of Americans for an Effective Presidency. At the suggestion
of the lower court, Common Cause took the issue of collusion to
the F.E.C., in September of 1980, and that is where it remained
as of the spring of 1983—a long time after the election. The
Carter-Mondale committee also brought a complaint, which
was also still pending. (The Reagan people took what opportunity they had to appoint to the F.E.C. people who share their
attitudes toward the campaign laws. Their first appointment
was Lee Ann Elliott, a former official of the American Medical
Association's political-action committee, AMPAC, which has had
its own run-ins with the limits of the federal election law.)

In congressional campaigns, independent committees try to
be helpful in a variety of ways. Direct mail has already been
mentioned. Another, of course, is to run television spots. The
independent committees look not for obvious winners, as corporate PACs do (at least in part), but for races where they might
make a difference. That is why the poll information is so important to them. Like the national committees, the independent
committees take advantage of the soft-money loophole, running
ads in an area which are ostensibly for the local party but are in
fact designed to help the national ticket. Dietrich says, "If
ninety percent of the candidates are for state and local office,
we can pay for ninety percent of the ad with corporate contribu-

tions—even though the ads are aimed at federal campaigns. So essentially it just wipes out the whole purpose of the F.E.C. The law just describes what you can't do. The TV commercials will never be allocated to a federal candidate, or, if so, it will only be a pittance. If you look up a congressman's report, you won't be able to tell that we had commercials pounding, pounding into his district. And it's perfectly legal—or within the letter of the law. All the independent PACs do the same thing. So we have a little dance which we dance around the law in a way that never breaks the letter but breaks the spirit of the law—but we don't agree with the law, anyway."

Much was made of the fact that the conservative independent committees—NCPAC and the Congressional Club—did not do so well at defeating targeted candidates for Congress in 1982 as they did in 1980. (The Fund for a Conservative Majority did slightly better.) In both years, the results were exaggerated. In 1980, the committees were a new phenomenon, and events were with them. By 1982, their presence in a campaign had become more of an issue, and events were against them. Now some liberal independent political-action committees have been established—and they, too, are using negative tactics. The real lesson of the 1982 campaign is not that independent committees are meaningless in congressional campaigns; it is that they will have to improve their tactics—and they probably will. Various proposals have been made for having the candidate on whose behalf an independent committee is working take responsibility for it. Others have been made that would go further, and abolish the committees, or cut back their role considerably, on the ground that they are devices for getting around the statutory limits on contributions. Some have argued that these committees are a vehicle for political expression and are therefore healthy. Others reply that what these committees are doing, and the scale on which they are doing it, goes beyond political expression—that they manipulate people's desire for political expression, and in a way that deliberately distorts the issues. And it is not as if these groups did not have an opportunity to express themselves through the political parties. They do; in fact, they have a large impact. They are not the same as grass-roots movements that form around an issue. These committees are highly skilled, directed organizations that use people's feelings about certain issues to gain influence. And now some right-wing groups (Richard Viguerie and his associates and the Fund for a Conservative Majority) are considering ways to use new communications technology—in particular, cable television—to make themselves into an even greater force.

There are things that can be done about the effect of money on our political system once the nature and the extent of the problem are recognized. The impact of the need for money on congressional behavior has been dramatic. First, there is no question that we have a political system in which politicians' access to money is vital and, in more cases than not, decisive. Richard Wirthlin, the Republican pollster, says, "Money not only can make the difference but can make a huge difference." He continues, "People make decisions based upon the way they see the world, and the way they see the world is conditioned by the information they have; and money can influence not only the information they have but also the perceptions they have, and therefore influences who wins and loses." Second, it is clear that the politicians' anxiety about having access to enough money corrodes, and even corrupts, the political system. It is clear that the effect on them is degrading and distracting at best. At the least, politicians increasingly consider how their votes will affect their own—and their opponents'—ability to raise money. At worst, votes are actually traded for money. It is clear that we are at some distance from the way the democratic process is supposed to work. The most fundamental question is, What kind of electoral process would give us the best kind of representation—the best at representing the public interest and producing public officials who, on the basis of experience and judgment, would make decisions that would not always represent passing public attitudes or be affected by financial contributions? Finally, it is clear that the system for funding Presidential campaigns with public money, in order to make them reasonably competitive and removed from the pressures of private interests, isn't working as it was intended to.

The broad outlines of what could be done to deal with all these things are: first, a system of public financing of congressional campaigns, which would include limits on what could be spent for the campaigns and a ceiling on the overall amount that any member could accept from political-action committees; second, a radical approach to political advertising, the costliest component of campaigns, which would include a ban on the purchase of air time and a provision for free air time; third, a reimposition of the limits on expenditures by independent committees, and other measures to close the loopholes being exploited by Presidential campaigns. Variations on all these proposals are possible, and objections to all of them are plentiful. Some of the proposals would be difficult to work out, but if the same amount of energy and ingenuity went into making the law effective that has gone into finding ways around it, the difficulties could be resolved. The point is not to try to establish a perfect political system but to try to get the system back closer to what it was intended to be.

Two of the proposals—those dealing with independent committees and political advertising—require some consideration of what the First Amendment is really about. Moreover, when the Supreme Court first ruled that limits on independent expenditures were unconstitutional, it found no history of abuse, which is understandable, since up to that point there were no limits on contributions. In the Buckley case, a prohibition on independent expenditures was held unconstitutional with only one dissenter—Justice Byron White. In its ruling in the Schmitt case, six years after Buckley, the Court was evenly divided on the question of independent expenditures by groups on behalf of publicly financed Presidential candidates, with one member unable to participate because of an apparent conflict of interest. Therefore, it would seem that the constitutional issue is no longer the settled question that people thought it was when the Court ruled in the Buckley case.

The Buckley decision was an odd one, because at the same time that it equated money with speech and held that limits on independent *expenditures* were unconstitutional, it held that limits on *contributions* to candidates were constitutional. Its rationale was that expenditures did not pose the same danger as contributions. But if one has an absolute right to spend unlimited amounts of money for a political candidate outside the candidate's campaign, why can't one contribute whatever one wants to the candidate? Archibald Cox, the professor of constitutional law at the Harvard Law School, who also served as Special Prosecutor during Watergate and is chairman of Common Cause, argued both the Buckley case and the Schmitt case, as well as other First Amendment cases before the Court. Cox says he thinks that it is at least a fifty-fifty possibility that all that the framers of the Constitution had in mind when they wrote the First Amendment was a prohibition on prior censorship, and that some people argue that the possibility is much greater. In any event, he says, one need not resort to that argument to get at the problem of the First Amendment and independent expenditures.

Cox explains the Court's apparent contradiction in the Buckley decision by saying he believes that what the Court had in mind when it considered independent expenditures was, say, a group of professors taking an ad in a newspaper, or an individual flying around the country making speeches in support of a candidate, or even someone buying fifteen or thirty minutes of television time on behalf of a candidate. Therefore, when Cox argued the Schmitt case he suggested that the Court could limit the effect of its finding in the Buckley case by stipulating that it was not thinking in terms of large organizations making independent expenditures, which they have funded by a money-raising effort, and which, as he pointed out, "even without consultation, it's no great trick to coordinate." He suggested that one way to deal with the proposition that spending money equals free speech would be to say that there are lots of different kinds of expenditures, and perhaps money is speech in the instance of a person spending money to publish or broadcast his own thoughts, while it is an entirely different thing when an organization raises money from all over the country and spends it to broadcast. The difference, he said, is that the money is collected nationally, and that it is used for much speech but few ideas. As for the Court's argument that independent expenditures do not create the risk of corrupting public policy, Cox replied that that may be true in the case of an individual who spends for his own personal expression, or of the group of professors, but it is not true in the case of groups that raise and spend millions on behalf of a candidate.

Cox suggests a new way of looking at our elections—a way that could be most helpful in clarifying our thinking about them. He says that an election ought to be treated like a town meeting or an argument before the Supreme Court. As he puts it, there are some forums where, to have meaningful, open debate, you see to it that everyone gets an equal allocation of time and a fair chance to express his point of view. "No one considers that a restriction on freedom of speech," Cox says.

If we redefine what we mean by "freedom of speech," and uncouple the idea of "the marketplace of ideas" from the idea of "the free market," we can begin to get back to how the political system was supposed to work. It is one thing to establish a system that guarantees contending factions an opportunity to express their views, and quite another to auction off the system to those factions that can afford to pay for the most time to express them—not to mention the secondary effects that such an auction system has. Whether or not the person who has the most broadcast time always prevails, it is demonstrable that the power and the cost of political broadcasting distort the political process.

A way to guarantee contending factions a chance to have their say, turn our elections into more of a fair fight, lower the amount of money that is spent on campaigns, and raise the level on which they are fought would be to prohibit political advertising and provide the candidates with free air time. This may sound like a radical concept, but in fact America is one of the very few countries in the world that allow any purchase of television time for political broadcasts; no Western European nation does. And, while we are at it, we could consider requiring that most of the free broadcast time be in segments of not less than, say, five or ten minutes. (In Great Britain, the major parties are currently required to broadcast in segments of a minimum of five or ten minutes.) This would make it necessary for candidates to actually say something, in contrast to the one-minute or thirty-second spots, which are uninformative at best and misleading at worst. (An argument has been made that you can tell what a candidate is like from his television spots, but that requires the public to be able to sort out fact from fiction when it doesn't necessarily have the information; and it puts the burden on the opponent to refute the spots—often something that cannot be done in thirty seconds or a minute. The answer is usually more complicated than the charge.) Arrangements would also have to be made to assure that the free time offered would be when people were likely to be watching—but this, too, could be worked out.

The essential point is that under this proposal the contenders would have a fair chance to be heard, without having to scramble to outspend their opponents for broadcasting—the most expensive and the most influential element of a campaign. Cox thinks that such a proposal could be upheld constitutionally. There would, of course, be stiff opposition to it. The broadcasters would oppose it, for obvious reasons; but the ownership of broadcasting stations is among the most lucrative businesses in America. A fallback position would be for the government to pay a portion of the cost of this broadcast time as part of a publicly financed system for congressional campaigns. (In effect, the government already does this for the publicly financed Presidential campaign.) But there is no point in adopting a fallback position until the fairest and most sensible plan has been tried. Whenever the idea of free broadcast time is brought up, a lot of sand is thrown in the air about such things as what to do in a media market like New York or Los Angeles, where there may be a number of races, or, alternatively, what to do in races where there are no media markets. Surely the mind of man can figure out some answer. When I was talking about this with Robert Dole, the chairman of the Senate Finance Committee, who, on the basis of what he had encountered in his efforts to write more equitable tax laws, is in favor of diminishing the role of money in campaigns, he said, "If they can figure out the tax code, they can figure this out." There are several paths of thinking that those trying to devise a solution might take. One is to keep in mind that the stations in the large media markets are among the most profitable ones. Another is that congressional candidates in areas like New York and Los Angeles often don't buy media time now, because they think it isn't worth it to pay for a broadcast that takes in so much more territory than their district. There is no particular reason that they should be given the means to start broadcasting where they did not do it before. But, in any case, they could be given air time without great financial risk to the stations. Another point to keep in mind is that cable television allows politicians to narrow the size of the audience they are trying to reach, and a number of politicians are already using cable, which is far less expensive than most traditional broadcast outlets. Or, in a media market with a number of candidates, the candidates could be given some free mailings instead. This, too, could be taken care of under a public financing scheme.

Common Cause has been advocating the granting of free response time to a candidate who has been attacked by an independent committee, its theory being that as long as such expenditures are allowed, this will neutralize the effect. If the attack came in the form of direct mail, the candidate could receive a subsidy to respond. But it is not out of the question that the courts will ban expenditures by the large-scale independent committees that have been springing up, especially if there is a system of public financing of congressional campaigns.

The idea of public financing of congressional campaigns has been gaining an increasing number of adherents. An aide to the House leadership said that what he witnessed during the consideration of the 1982 tax-increase bill had made him a convert to the idea. When I asked him why, specifically, he replied, "The long lines of suitors and the access they had." A number of people believed that the Ninety-seventh Congress reflected the impact of the pressure of money, in its various forms, more than any Congress before it. And this sense of things led a number of people who had never before subscribed to the idea of public financing of congressional campaigns to decide that the system had to be changed. A former member of Congress said to me recently, "I used to be against public financing. I thought raising money was an important way to build a campaign, to get people committed. But then I began to see how the present system was corrupting even the best of them on the Hill. And they gin each other up: they see that others are doing it, and say, Why not? It became very depressing to watch. And I changed my mind about public financing." Actually, the public-financing schemes would still allow for private participation.

A number of proposals for a system of public financing have been put forward by members of Congress as well as by Common Cause. They have been sponsored by both Republicans and Democrats. They have several common characteristics. They would provide, for the candidates in the general election, a matching system similar to that which obtains in the Presidential-primary system, and would impose spending limits. (The question of public financing of congressional primaries has been set aside as something to be worked out, if necessary, once a system for the general elections is in place.) It is possible to consider spending limits without a public-financing system, but this, too, would require a change of opinion on the part of the Supreme Court; and there would always be the problem of setting the limits high enough to make candidates viable and low enough to give them a chance of not being utterly at the mercy of contributors and fund raisers. Just as the Presidential-primary system matches private individual contributions of two hundred and fifty dollars, the congressional system would match contributions of a hundred dollars. A bill sponsored by David Obey, a Democratic representative from Wisconsin and a late convert to the idea of public financing, would limit to ninety thousand dollars the total amount of matching money for a candidate for the House. Individuals would still be allowed to contribute a thousand dollars. Some of those who favor public financing would consider allowing higher individual contributions in exchange for an agreement on such a scheme. The proposals for public financing also contain a limit on the total amount a candidate could accept from political-action committees. So private money would not be driven out of the congressional campaigns—it would just be brought under control. And members of Congress would be freed from the anxiety and fear—and corruption—that accompany the present race for money. Obey's bill would limit to ninety thousand dollars the amount that candidates for the House could accept from PACS. His bill does not deal with Senate races, but others have proposed setting limits for Senate races on the basis of a state's population. A bill sponsored by Representatives Mike Synar, Democrat of Oklahoma; Jim Leach, Republican of Iowa; and Dan Glickman, Democrat of Kansas, would limit the amount that House candidates could accept from PACS to seventy-five thousand dollars, while the amount that Senate candidates could accept would vary with the size of the state—from seventy-five thousand to five hundred thousand. But the problem with simply limiting the amount that can be received from PACS, without dealing with the larger context, is that the interests that give through PACS would simply turn around and give through individual contributions—as independent oil largely does now. Common Cause and some people on Capitol Hill would also lower the amount that a PAC could contribute to an individual: from ten thousand dollars per election cycle—five thousand for the primary and five thousand for the general election—to half that amount. Obey's bill would limit campaign spending in a congressional general election to a hundred and eighty thousand dollars—a figure that seems unrealistically low and appears to be a negotiating position. The bill would also limit personal and immediate-family expenditures to twenty thousand dollars for those who participate in the public-financing plan. If a candidate chose not to accept public financing but to spend large amounts of his own money, or to exceed the spending limits, the spending limits on his opponent would be lifted, and the opponent would receive double the amount in matching funds. Obey would provide free television time for a candidate to respond to an independent group's attack, or additional public financing equal to the amount of the independent expenditures for television; and he would also offer to match other independent expenditures that amounted in the aggregate to more than five thousand dollars.

If in fact there would remain imbalances as a result of labor's efforts to get people registered and to the polls, it is not beyond the mind of man to figure out a solution to this, either. (It is to be remembered that both labor and business are now allowed to spend unlimited amounts to communicate with their own members or employees on political matters. Moreover, such organizations as the Chamber of Commerce conduct get-out-the-vote drives, and business is developing other ways to compete with labor.) The possibilities range from prohibiting these activities—which doesn't seem very healthy—to improving the registration system or designing a system under which the parties play the major role in these activities. One possibility would be to allow the parties to raise money for such activities (as was done in 1979 for the Presidential campaign)—and, in both Presidential and congressional campaigns, to impose limits and an effective reporting system. This way, soft money could be brought under control, and the two problems would be dealt with at once.

Two arguments made against public financing are that it would amount to an incumbent-protection act, since incumbents enjoy certain advantages, and that it would guarantee a challenger enough money to give an incumbent a disconcertingly stiff race. (The second argument is one that people on Capitol Hill make very quietly.) Both arguments, of course, can't be true. And if public financing amounted to an incumbent-protection act, it would have passed long since, unless Congress is an uncommonly noble institution. Moreover, most of the public-financing schemes have taken it into account that a highly restrictive spending limit would prevent challengers from competing effectively. Fred Wertheimer, the president of Common Cause, points out that the first two incumbent Presidents to run under the system of public financing of Presidential campaigns—Ford and Carter—both lost. As for the advantages of incumbency, Common Cause has brought legal action against abuse of the franking privilege. Wertheimer adds, "Incumbency has its pluses and its minuses." He says, "The key is to have a system that allows a challenger to compete. That's really all we can do, and that's all we should do."

Leach refers to the proposal to limit PAC contributions as "a kind of domestic SALT agreement between big business and big labor." In introducing his bill, Obey said, "We do not object to people accepting PAC contributions. But the size of these contributions moved around the nation by unseen hands in Washington office buildings can determine the politics of Wisconsin or Montana or Vermont or any other state in the Union. We do object to that." The lines between the representative and his constituents have been disturbed, if not yet completely cut. Elections are determined in increasing measure by forces outside the district and the state.

A number of Republicans think that it is not against the interests of their party to support a public-financing system. Barber Conable, a Republican representative from New York, who is among them, says, "Large contributions tend to come to incumbents; by the nature of things, our party will have more challengers." One Republican political consultant says, "Republicans who oppose public financing—and the great majority do—say, 'How can we overcome the numerical disadvantage of being a Republican?' I don't think that's a valid objection. It is true that

Republicans are in the minority, but that is not an argument for opposing public financing. Privately, their argument is 'We can blow them out by outspending them.' My view is that if the money represents an unfair advantage it ought to be eliminated. Where is the ethics or morality in saying the system ought to be maintained because it benefits you, if the advantage is inherently unfair?"

It has been argued that the public financing of congressional campaigns would be costly. However, most of the proposals call for it to be paid for out of the voluntary dollar checkoff on tax returns, which might be raised to two dollars—so the system would be self-financed. Another dollar a year seems a small price to pay. (One estimate, based on recent campaign costs, is that the system would cost about eighty million dollars per two-year election cycle.) The more important point is how expensive it is *not* to have public financing and some limit on PAC contributions, and how risky it is *not* to restore the Presidential-election system to the way it was supposed to work. The costs are everywhere—throughout the tax code and the federal budget. They turn up in everything from the Pentagon budget to medical bills. In effect, as we go about our daily lives, buying food, gasoline, and medicine, and as we pay our taxes, we are paying for the current system of financing campaigns.

And there are less tangible but more important costs. We are paying in the declining quality of politicians and of the legislative product, and in the rising public cynicism. We have allowed it to become increasingly difficult for the good people who remain in politics to function well. What results is a corrosion of the system and a new kind of squalor—conditions that are well known to those who are in it and to those who deal with it at close range. The public knows that something is very wrong. As the public cynicism gets deeper, the political system gets worse. Until the problem of money is dealt with, the system will not get better. We have allowed the basic idea of our democratic process—representative government—to slip away. The only question is whether we are serious about trying to retrieve it.

INDEX

INDEX

Accountants, 71
Advertising, 7–8, 147, 149–151
Aerospace industry, 71
Agricultural industry, 71
All-Savers Certificates, 46
Ambassadorial appointments, 1–2,
    122–124
American Dental Association, 81
American Federation of Labor–
    Congress of Industrial Organiza-
    tions (A.F.L.-C.I.O.), 9, 36, 100
American Medical Association
    (A.M.A.), 8, 11, 32, 73, 81–82,
    143
American Political Report, 137
Americans for an Effective Presi-
    dency, 140–141, 143
Americans for Change, 139–141
American Telephone & Telegraph
    (A.T.&T.), 71–72, 89
Amway Corporation, 30, 35
Anderson, Stan, 104
Annenberg, Walter H., 122–123
Anthony, Beryl, 44
Antitrust laws, 85–86, 88
Askew, Reubin, 100
Assets-and-priorities group, 23
Association of Trial Lawyers of
    America, 64
Atwater, Lee, 23–25, 27, 29
Automobile industry, 71

Baker, Bobby, 3
Baker, Howard, 126
Banking industry, 7, 60, 86
Bankruptcy Improvements Act, 86
Baron, Alan, 137

Bentsen, Lloyd, 40
Bidding war, 38, 43, 46, 113
Bingham, Jonathan, 95
Bloomingdale, Alfred, 115
Boggs, Thomas, 59–64, 66, 88–89
Bond, Richard, 16, 23, 26, 55
Boren, David, 39–40
Brewing industry, 85–86
Briscoe, Dolph, 40
Brock, William, 20, 108
Brouse, J. Robert, 35
Brown, Jerry, 18, 21
Buckley, Charles, 95
Buckley, James, 121, 135
Buckley v. Valeo, 10, 18, 95,
    134–135, 142, 147–148
Budde, Bernadette, 31–33, 81
Bumpers, Dale, 96, 98
Bundling, 13
Burch, Dean, 88
Bush, George, 24, 55, 107, 115, 125,
    128
Business-Industry Political Action
    Committee (BIPAC), 9–10, 29–34,
    54, 74
Byrd, Robert, 57, 64

Cabinet appointments, 120–122
Cable television, 72, 151
Caddell, Patrick, 97, 102, 139
California, 17–18, 21, 104, 107
Campaign America, 62, 87
Campaign costs, 4, 94
Campbell, Carroll, 76
Carter, Jimmy, 39–40, 47–48, 82, 101,
    116, 118, 124, 134, 142, 155
Carter-Mondale committee, 143

Casey, Bill, 137
Cash contributions, limit on, 10
Chamber of Commerce, 10, 31–32, 37, 53–54, 154
Chemical industry, 21, 71
Chennault, Anna, 140
Children's contributions, 119
Chiles, H.E. (Eddie), 112
Chrysler Corporation, 63–64
Citizens for the Republic, 128–129
Clean Air Act, 32, 89
Clements, William, 107, 140
Coalition for a New Beginning, 114
Coelho, Tony, 41–44, 46, 48–49, 87
Committee for the Survival of a Free Congress, 116
Committee on Political Education (COPE), 9, 36
Commodities trading, 71, 86–87
Common Cause, 8, 10, 70, 82, 86, 142–143, 148, 151–153, 155
Communications Act (1934), 72
Communications industry, 71
Communications Workers of America, 36
Computer Assisted Telephone Interviewing (CATI), 55
Computer industry, 71
Conable, Barber, 44, 155
Congress, effect of money on function of, 2–5, 20–22, 78–92
Congressional campaigns, 1–2, 7–11, 15, 17, 23–29, 33–34, 94–95, 139, 143–144, 147, 152–156
Congressional Club, 126, 133–134, 136–137, 141, 144
Congressional committees, 67–76, 82–83
Congressional members' contributions to colleagues, 69–70, 71
Connally, John, 101, 120, 125, 128
Construction industry, 71
Consultants, 138–139
Coors, Joseph, 112, 116, 131
Coors family, 115–116

Corporate contributions, 1, 6–11, 13–16, 20, 28–35, 38–52, 70, 78, 96, 104–106, 114, 143
Corporate taxes, 38–39, 41–43, 46
Corruption, 95–98
Corrupt Practices Act (1925), 7, 10
Cotton interests, 71
Cox, Archibald, 148–150
Craig, Earle, 115
Cranston, Alan, 43, 49
Craver, Roger, 133
Culver, John, 21, 77

Dairy industry, 9, 71
D'Amato, Alfonse, 19
Dart, Justin, 78, 112, 114–116, 123, 131
Debts, campaign, 14
Delegates, convention, contributions to, 120
Democratic Business Council, 63
Democratic Party, 16–18, 36–37, 39–45, 116
  congressional campaigns, 19, 26
  direct-mail fund-raising, 27, 131–133
  fund-raisers, 58, 61, 65, 119–120, 124–125
  PACS, 20–21, 35–36, 100
  Presidential campaigns, 102–103, 108–110, 116–118, 142
  search for business money, 38–52
Dentists, 71. See also American Dental Association
Depletion allowance, 39
Deukmejian, George, 17
DeVos, Richard, 30–31
Dietrich, Paul, 105, 132–133, 136–137, 143–144
Direct-mail attacks on candidates, 151
Direct-mail fund-raising, 27, 130–133, 138–139
Direct Selling Association, 35, 92
Distinguished Presidential Support Certificate, 129

Doctors, 71. *See also* American Medical Association
Dole, Robert, 43, 62–63, 87, 96, 126, 151
Domestic content bill, 86
Donovan, Raymond, 120–122
Downey, Thomas, 45, 79
Drug companies, 71

Eagles (Republican), 110, 113
Education, Department of, 36, 118
Edwards, James, 140
Eisenhower Center, 106
Eizenstat, Stuart, 62, 88
Election laws, 1, 3, 7–10, 12–16, 18, 33–34, 99–107, 142
Electronics industry, 71
Elliott, Lee Ann, 143
Energy industry, 71
Engineers, 71
Environmental issues, 21, 37, 71, 75, 89, 91

Federal Election Commission (F.E.C.), 10, 12–14, 18, 67, 101–102, 106, 115, 121–122, 128–129, 135, 143
Federalist Papers, The, 6
Federal Trade Commission (F.T.C.), 78, 80–81
Fenwick, Millicent, 95
Ferris, Charles, 77, 88
Financial industry, 71
Finkelstein, Arthur, 138
First Amendment issues, 135, 147–148
Flanigan, Peter, 140
Florida, 104
Fluor, J. Robert, 30
Foley, Thomas, 87, 116
Food industry, 71
Ford, Gerald R., 123, 135, 141, 155
Forgotson, Edward, 40
Frenzel, Bill, 69
Fund for a Conservative Majority, 105, 136–138, 141, 144–145

Fund-raisers, 57–61, 64–66, 69, 117–118

General Electric, 62–63
Gephardt, Richard, 41–42, 44, 46, 49–51, 82, 116
Gerrity, Ned, 62
Get-out-the-vote drives, 36–37, 104, 154
Glickman, Dan, 153
Goldwater, Barry, 125, 130
Government regulations, 55
Grain interests, 71
Grassley, Charles, 21
Gray, Robert, 88, 113
Great Britain, 150
Gun lobby, 71

Hance, Kent, 68, 93
Hanna, Mark, 7
Hard money, 15, 142
Harriman, Averell, 58, 106
Hart, Gary, 100
Hauser, Gustave, 73
Helms, Jesse, 126, 133–134, 136, 138
High-technology industry, 47, 50
Holland, Ken, 48, 68, 76
Hollings, Ernest, 126
Holtzman, Elizabeth, 19
Hospital industry, 71, 82
House Agriculture Committee, 87
House elections, 25–26
House Energy and Commerce Committee, 67–68, 70–72, 74–75, 89
House Foreign Affairs Committee, 68
House Interior and Insular Affairs Committee, 74
House Judiciary Committee, 68, 85
House Merchant Marine and Fisheries Committee, 85
House of Representatives, 11, 38, 44, 85–87, 153
House Ways and Means Committee, 38, 43–45, 47, 66–69, 76, 83
Humphrey, Hubert, 142
Hunt, James, 133

Illinois, 17, 104
Inaugural Trust Fund, 113
Independent committees, 99, 108,
    115, 123, 134–145, 147–148, 151
Individual contributions, 12, 14, 16,
    104–105, 109–110, 114, 119–120,
    125, 142
Inouye, Daniel, 2, 78
Insurance industry, 71
International Communication
    Agency, 111
International Telephone and Tele-
    graph Corporation, 62
Iowa, 34

Johnson, Lyndon B., 39
Jones, James, 41
Jorgensen, Earle, 115

Kansas, 112
Keefe, Robert, 14, 99, 105, 109, 117
Keene, David, 135, 139
Kemp, Jack, 126
Kennedy, Edward, 126
Kennelly, Barbara, 76
Kerr, Robert, 39
Kline, Richard, 41–43
Kling, S. Lee, 49, 64

Labor unions, 8–11, 13, 16, 36,
    70–71, 75, 86, 96, 100, 102–104,
    109, 117, 154
La Follette, Robert, 7
Landow, Nathan, 124–125
Lawyer-lobbyists, 57–66, 87–88
Lawyers' contributions to PACS, 66, 71
Laxalt, Paul, 136
Leach, Jim, 34, 98, 131, 153, 155
Levitas, Elliott, 81–82, 116
Lobbyists' Superbowl, 88
Loeb, John, Jr., 123
Long, Gillis, 41, 70
Long, Russell, 64
Lott, Trent, 54, 56
Louis, John J., 122–123
Lugar, Richard, 87

Lyon, James, 112

McCandless, Robert, 59
McCann, William, 122
McCarthy, Eugene, 135
McGovern, George, 142
MacGregor, Clark, 27–28
McKevitt, James, 91
McKinley, William, 7
McMillian, John, 49
Machinery industry, 71
Malt Beverage Interbrand Competi-
    tion Act, 85–86
Manatt, Charles, 38, 63
Mansfield, Mike, 57
Maritime unions, 118
Mathews, Tom, 133
Media consultants, 138
Medical products suppliers, 71, 82
Metal industry, 71
Metzenbaum, Howard, 62, 85
Michel, Robert, 17, 69
Michigan, 102–103
Milk industry, 71
Miller, James, 81
Mining, 71
Missouri, 104
Mondale, Walter, 100, 126
Moral Majority, 116
Mosbacher, Robert, 111
Motion picture industry, 62, 88
Mott, Stewart, 131, 135
Moyers, Bill, 49
Murdock, David, 112
Murray, Vera, 65

National Association for Association
    Political Action Committees
    (NAFAPAC), 34–35, 92
National Association of Business
    Political Action Committees
    (NABPAC), 35
National Association of Home
    Builders, 31, 54
National Association of Manufac-
    turers (N.A.M.), 9, 30–31

National Association of Realtors, 11,
32, 35, 54, 73, 92–93
National Committee for an Effective
Congress, 129
National Conservative Political Ac-
tion Committee (NCPAC), 64, 134,
137–139, 141, 144
National Education Association
(N.E.A.), 36, 100, 118
National Federation of Independent
Business (N.F.I.B.), 54, 90–91
Nationalization of campaigns, 33–34
National Organization for Women, 91
National Republican Congressional
Committee, 11, 26
Natural gas, 40, 49, 62
Nevada, 25
New York, 104, 107, 125
New York Civil Liberties Union, 135
Nixon, Richard, 1, 8, 105, 122–123,
142
Nofziger, Lyn, 53–54, 106, 111, 129,
137–138
North Carolina, 133
Nuclear-freeze movement, 37
Nurses, 71

Obey, David, 21–22, 33, 52, 90,
153–154
O'Connor, Pat, 62
O'Connor, Sandra Day, 143
Oil industry, 14, 21, 39–45, 50, 62,
91, 112, 114–115
Oklahoma, 112, 114
O'Leary, Brad, 140

PAC Manager, The, 30
PACs. See Political-action committees
Panetta, Leon, 21–22
Paper industry, 71
Pennsylvania, 104
Perkins, Robert, 103–105, 111–113
Phillips, Kevin, 137
Pipeline, natural gas, 49
Plunkitt, George Washington, 95

Political-action committees (PACS),
8–14, 20–21, 24–27, 29–30,
34–36, 40–41, 52, 59–61, 66–68,
70–76, 85–86, 90, 92, 99–100,
116, 126–129, 153, 155
Polls, 55, 136–138, 143
Poultry and livestock industry, 71
Presidential campaigns, 1–2, 9, 15,
99–108, 111–117, 119–129,
134–143, 147
Presidential candidates' PACS, 71,
126–129
Presidential inauguration (1980),
113–114
Preyer, Richardson, 70
Professional associations, 8, 34, 141
Public Citizen, 81
Public financing of campaigns, 1, 7,
9, 11, 52, 95, 100–101, 135, 142,
143, 147, 150, 151, 152–156

Rabb, Maxwell, 122
Radaker, Byron, 38, 63
Railsback, Tom, 33
Rayburn, Sam, 39
Reagan, Ronald, 24, 36–37, 101, 103,
107, 113, 115, 120–125, 128–129,
131, 134–142
Real estate industry, 71. See also Na-
tional Association of Realtors
Record industry, 88
Reed, Thomas, 140
Regan, Don, 24
Regulatory agencies, 80–81
Report cards, of congressmen, 90–92
Republican Party, 7, 16–19, 28–31,
40–41, 53–56, 91, 103, 106,
138–139, 142, 155–156
congressional campaigns, 19,
25–27
direct-mail fund-raising, 27,
130–132
fund-raisers, 120–125
PACS, 20–21, 24, 35
Presidential campaigns, 101–116,
142

White House coordination of political money, 23–27
Retail businesses, 62, 71, 86
Reuss, Henry, 96
Riegle, Donald, 87
Rodino, Peter, 85
Rollins, Edward, 23
Roosevelt, Theodore, 7
Ross, Steven, 47, 124
Rostenkowski, Dan, 41–42, 44, 68–69, 78, 93, 116
Roth, William, 87
Rubenstein, David, 88
Rudman, Warren, 81
Russo, Marty, 87

Saeman, John, 72
Safe-harbor tax provision, 39, 63
Savings-and-loan industry, 46, 86
Schmitt, Harrison, 139–140, 142, 147
Sears, John, 107, 125
Securities and Exchange Commission, 86, 124
Securities industry, 60, 72, 86
Senate, 44, 87, 153
Senate Agriculture Committee, 87
Senate Banking Committee, 60
Senate Committee on Commerce, Science, and Transportation, 67
Senate elections, 25, 153
Senate Finance Committee, 67
Service industries, 71
Shad, John, 124
Shannon, James, 42, 44–45, 51–52
Sharp, Philip, 74–76
Shelby, Rick, 24, 27, 29
Shipping industry, 85
Shorenstein, Walter, 49
Silverman, Leon, 121
Sinnott, Nancy, 25
Soft money, 14–18, 26, 55, 92, 99, 102–106, 108–109, 111–113, 116–117, 127–128, 142–143, 154
Speaker's Club, 49
Special-interest groups, 6, 84–92, 97–98

Speech, freedom of, 10, 135, 147, 148–149
Spencer, Stuart, 140–141
Stark, Thomas, 66
State parties, 15–17, 101–102, 106–107, 142
Steel industry, 71
Stock options, 46
Stone, Roger, 138
Stone, W. Clement, 1
Strauss, Robert, 40, 43, 49, 64–66, 88–89, 117
Sugar industry, 60, 71
Supreme Court rulings, 10, 18, 134–135, 142–143, 147–149
Synar, Mike, 89, 91, 153

Tammany Hall, 95
Tauke, Tom, 34
Tax legislation, 38–39, 41–47, 55, 62–63, 92, 113, 152
Telecommunications industry, 72–73, 89
Television advertising, 7–8, 137–138, 143–144, 147, 149–151
Texas, 104, 107–108, 112, 114–115, 120
Textile industry, 71, 76
Thaxton, Richard, 35, 92–93
Tillman Act (1907), 7
Timmons, William, 27–30, 64, 104, 106, 108, 113
Tobacco industry, 71
Trade associations, 8, 11, 13, 34–35
Transition Foundation, 113
Transportation industry, 71
Tuttle, Holmes, 112, 114–116, 123

Udall, Morris, 126
United Auto Workers, 36, 86, 102
United Steelworkers, 36
Used-car dealers, 78–80

Valenti, Jack, 62, 88
Vander Jagt, Guy, 11
Videotaping, home, 88

Viguerie, Richard, 133, 138, 145
von Damm, Helene, 123
Voter education and registration, 104, 117

Walker, Charls, 63
Wall Street Journal, 55, 59
Warner Communications, 47, 73, 124
Wasserman, Lew, 49, 88, 124–125
Waxman, Henry, 70
Welch, Ted, 111
Werblin, Sonny, 121
Wertheimer, Fred, 10, 155

Wexford, 113
Wexler, Anne, 88
White, Byron, 147
White House, coordination of political money, 23–27
Wick, Charles, 111–114
Williams, J. D., 61–63, 88
Wilson, Charles, 41–42
Wilson, Pete, 17, 21
Winograd, Morley, 102
Wirth, Tim, 71–73
Wirthlin, Richard, 55, 99, 108, 137, 146
Wright, Jim, 70, 87

ABOUT THE AUTHOR

Elizabeth Drew is a regular contributor to *The New Yorker*, and since June 1973 has been a television commentator for Post-Newsweek stations and appears frequently on "Agronsky & Company." She also participates in "Meet the Press" and "Face the Nation." *Politics and Money* is a fuller and updated version of a *New Yorker* series for which Ms. Drew received the prestigious Sidney Hillman Award. She is the author of four other books: *Washington Journal: The Events of 1973-74*; *American Journal: The Events of 1976*; *Senator*; and *Portrait of an Election: The 1980 Presidential Campaign*.

Born in Cincinnati, Ohio, Elizabeth Drew graduated Phi Beta Kappa from Wellesley College, where she majored in political science. She then worked as an associate editor for *The Writer* in Boston. From 1959 to 1964 she was a writer and editor for *Congressional Quarterly* in Washington, and in 1964 began writing for such journals as the *Atlantic* and the *New York Times Magazine*. From 1967 until 1973 she was Washington editor for *Atlantic Monthly*.

Ms. Drew has received many awards for her work and holds honorary degrees from six universities, including Yale, Reed, Georgetown, and Williams. She has been described by Dan Wakefield as "the American Boswell" and in her Georgetown citation as "the Samuel Pepys of Washington."